THE MUSLIM GUIDE

For Teachers, Employers, Community and Social Administrators in Britain

Mustafa Yusuf McDermott
Muhammad Manazir Ahsan

THE ISLAMIC FOUNDATION

Revised Edition 1986/1406 H.
Second Revised Edition 1993/1413 H.

ISBN 0 86037 057 7 (paperback)
ISBN 0 86037 061 5 (hardback)

Published by
The Islamic Foundation,
Markfield Dawah Centre,
Ratby Lane,
Markfield,
Leicester LE67 9RN,
United Kingdom.

Quran House,
P.O. Box 30611,
Nairobi,
Kenya.

P.M.B. 3193,
Kano,
Nigeria.

Printed by The Cromwell Press,
Broughton Gifford, Melksham,
Wiltshire SN12 8PH

بسم الله الرحمن الرحيم

Contents

Foreword

This book presents a brief outline of the religion and culture of Islam. There are many Muslims in Britain who now constitute an integral part of our multi-racial and multi-cultural society. They are a vigorous community, with strong internal bonds.

However, there is widespread ignorance about this religious group. Islam is a way of life, with firm and clear views on a variety of issues such as hygiene, diet, education, the role of women and, indeed, life after death. The daily lives of Muslims, their manners and mores are all determined by these views. It is, therefore, inevitable that their cultural practices and beliefs should occasionally be thought of as being incompatible with the traditional patterns of behaviour within the host society. But more often than not this incompatibility arises out of ignorance and lack of communication rather than because of the unwillingness of Muslims to come to terms with existing institutions. This ignorance has also tended to create a series of myths which, like any myths, project a completely erroneous view about the religion of Islam. These two factors – lack of knowledge and the propagation of myths – can have a serious effect on the relationship between Muslims and other communities in our society. This book is therefore welcome not only because of the substantive information which it contains, but also because it will go some way towards increasing the level of knowledge about Muslims in British society.

As such, it should be of great value to teachers, employers, community workers and administrators, who in their daily work come face to face with members of the Muslim community. I should also underline the need for sympathy and understanding in enabling Muslims to live alongside other communities in peace and harmony in our multi-cultural society and thus to play their part as full citizens.

The Commission for Racial Equality has the duty, among others, to promote good and harmonious relations between persons of different racial and cultural backgrounds. My colleagues and I regard factual information such as that contained in this book as an important means of achieving that objective.

David Lane
Chairman, Commission
for Racial Equality

Foreword

The phenomenon of a pluralistic society, which today confronts Britain and many other countries, East and West, is not something new in man's history. Indeed the flow of human migration, from one part of the world to another, in waves large and small, has been a common and recurrent feature in history. Sometimes the propelling force has been a new ideological and cultural mission; sometimes the quest for new land and a better life; sometimes flight from wars and famine and the search for sanctuary and food; sometimes naked conquest and expansion. In all cases, the result has been a cross-fertilisation of ideas, cultures and races. Indeed, migration has been one of the major forces responsible for the development of human civilisation.

The needs of post-war economic reconstruction, the dissolution of empires and the availability of faster and cheaper means of travel, among many other reasons, have resulted in the influx of a sizeable immigrant population into Britain and other European countries like France and Germany. A significant proportion of them are Muslims, who have made these countries their homes. Muslims are always characterised by their strong desire and endeavour to live by Islam. For Islam is unique among religions in that it claims to be a total way of life for humanity. This naturally raises certain problems when Muslims are placed in a different cultural environment, and yet wish to practise their religion and preserve their cultural identity. They are prepared to contribute towards the growth of an integrated society, where each culture will have full room to preserve itself and to flourish. But what they would find impossible to accept is to assimilate and lose themselves in their newly found home.

Those in positions of responsibility who have occasion to

deal with Muslims in various settings – at home, at school, at work, in hospital, in court, in penal institutions or in many other similar situations – need not necessarily look upon the task of meeting Muslim cultural requirements as vexing and burdensome. With a little thought and care, they will prove not only simple and easy to meet but a challenge and a pleasure to learn and respect. Learning and accommodating in diversity and pluralism bring their own rewards, as each culture has much to offer another.

It is to bring joy and happiness to both non-Muslims and Muslims in various situations of cross-cultural contact that the Islamic Foundation has prepared this brief Muslim Guide for all those responsible for dealing with Muslims. I hope this will greatly facilitate the task of all who want to know more about their Muslim neighbour/classmate/workmate/patient/ward etc., etc., in order to help him live by his religion. Though the book is primarily intended for teachers, employers and community and social administrators in Britain, I trust that it will prove equally useful to people in similar situations in other Western countries where sizeable Muslim populations have now come to exist, especially in Germany, France, Scandinavia and the U.S.A. We shall consider our effort more than amply rewarded if, in even one single human situation, this book succeeds through promoting respect and accommodation in bringing comfort and happiness to two people. For happiness is such a scarce commodity in a world tormented with conflict, tension, prejudice and bigotry.

I am grateful to my brothers and colleagues who have borne the responsibility of preparing this book, in particular to Dr. M.M. Ahsan for preparing the first draft, to Brother Mustafa McDermott for revising it as co-author in collaboration with Dr. Ahsan, to Brother Mashuq Ally for working closely with both of them in finalising the manuscript, and to Brother Muhtar Holland for reading it finally and offering many helpful suggestions.

We pray to God to bless our humble efforts with His mercy and acceptance.

23 Muḥarram 1400
12 December 1979

Khurram Jah Murad
Director General

Authors' Preface

At conferences, and in the course of general conversations, many members of the host community have expressed a need for a brief outline of the religion and culture of Islam, based specifically upon the religious and social problems which confront the Muslim at school, at work and in the community. This modest book is a response to those genuine requests for information on problems in which we have a mutual interest in trying to solve. Educational achievement, the organisational efficiency of industry and peaceful relations in the community are dependent on the understanding, co-operation and tolerance of all people brought together in the execution of common objectives and nationwide harmony and progress.

The purpose of this Guide is to provide teachers, employers, trade union officials, social administrators and community workers with an outline of Islamic religion and culture. It is also intended to assist them in their everyday contact with members of the Muslim community in Britain.

Minority communities in Britain have usually enjoyed a high degree of religious tolerance. The Roman Catholic and Jewish communities provide two excellent examples of religious co-existence, and creditably reflect the co-operation of the Government and responsible authority in all spheres of their community life. But help and co-operation from educational, industrial and social service organisations also depends upon the information that the Muslim minority groups are prepared to make available. Responsible authority has the difficult task of running their organisations efficiently on the one hand, and creating harmony on the other in this increasingly plural society. With racial harmony and religious freedom very much in mind, we have taken the liberty of publishing this Guide on behalf of the 1.5 million Muslims living, learning and working in Britain. We sincerely hope that this Guide will prove helpful and provide the basis for further discussion, the resolution of current problems and the formulation of effective socio-religious policies, within and outside the Muslim community in Britain.

Various brothers and colleagues from inside and outside the Foundation helped us in the preparation of the Guide with their suggestions and comments. We are specially grateful to Dr. A.F.A. Sayeed, O.B.E., for his general help and professional advice on the medical section and the executive members of the Muslim Teachers Association for helpful suggestions relating to the education of Muslim children. We are also indebted to Brother Khurram Murad, Director General of the Foundation, and Mr. David Lane, Chairman, Race Relations Commission, for writing the foreword for this book. Last, but not least, we would like to mention our colleague, Brother Mashuq Ally, who not only took a keen interest in this work, but offered helpful suggestions for improvement. We hope that readers will assist us by giving their comments and suggestions.

1st Muḥarram, 1400 — **M. Y. McDermott**
November 20, 1979 — **M.M. Ahsan**

Preface to the Second Revised Edition

Several new organisations have been formed and many addresses have changed since this book was first published in 1980. In this second revised edition, we have provided the new addresses, added a list of Muslim full-time schools, relief organisations and updated the list of mosques and organisations. This book is being used as recommended course material for the Cultural Awareness courses (see Appendix V) run by the Education and Training Unit of the Islamic Foundation.

Shawwāl 1413 H
April 1993 — **Editors**

1

Muslims in Britain: An Introduction

Origin and Basis

The religion of the 1.5 million Muslims living in Britain is Islam, a religion followed by over a billion Muslims spread throughout the world. The Muslim community in Britain is predominantly Asian, immigrants from Pakistan, India, Bangladesh and East Africa; yet, in much smaller groups, there are Muslims from Cyprus, Turkey, the Middle East, Africa, Malaysia and Indonesia who are also permanently settled here in employment and business. In addition, there is an increasing "floating" population of Muslim university students, English language pupils, visiting businessmen and tourists drawn from various nationalities. Nevertheless, in terms of numbers, cultural predominance, national identity and interrelationship with the host community, the Muslim community is, and is seen to be, largely Asian, characterised not only by national allegiance, but also by strongly entrenched provincial and village loyalties and variations in language, custom, dress, etc.

Islam is, however, and will always remain, the key to the understanding of the Muslim way of life, their culture, customs and practices and the issues and problems that arise at the level of cross-cultural contacts. The fact that Islam is *not merely a religion*, but a guidance and way of life for the totality of human existence – spiritual or physical, religious or political, individual or societal – has been the most important factor in shaping the Muslim community. The crucial role of Islam in Muslim life must be properly understood by all those who are involved in any relationship with Muslims in Britain.

Distribution

The Muslim community is unevenly scattered throughout Britain, but mainly concentrated in the industrial cities and towns of the South, the Midlands and the North. Muslim students appear to be well represented in all the universities and colleges in Britain. English language pupils, particularly in the private sector of the British education system, tend to be concentrated in London, the seaside resorts of the South coast and the traditional "olde" cities such as Oxford, Cambridge, Norwich and Bath. Muslim tourists are mostly found in London.

Structure and Status

In the mid-fifties and early sixties, the Muslim community in Britain appeared to be predominantly male and of working age, coming to this country for working spells of two or three years before returning home to settle down. Now, however, their age and sex distribution tend to follow the demographic pattern of the host community, and even though Muslim families have more children, there is considerable evidence to indicate that the average size of Muslim families in Britain is decreasing.

This reflects the Muslim community in Britain not, as is the case of the "guest workers" in Germany, as a mere transient supplementary working force of manual labourers; but as an integrated community of immigrants working in factories, transport, Local Government, the Civil Service, the professions and as self-employed in private enterprises, ranging from the corner shop to ultra-modern factories and chain stores. They have made Britain their home; they are prepared to contribute fully to its prosperity; but they should also receive full facilities to live as Muslims, as they would in their own home country.

The Muslim community today is composed of two distinct generations and a third generation is quietly emerging. The second and third generation of Muslims are likely to be well educated, fluent in English and well integrated with the host community, but nonetheless obligated and loyal to their religion – Islam.

Family Structure

The family is central to the whole scheme of social life envisaged by Islam. It must be preserved and strengthened at all costs. This concern is the source of numerous regulations prescribed by Islam, like those regarding the relationship between the sexes and their intermingling, punishments for extra-marital sex, dress and many other similar things. The strength of the family institution is also responsible for the strong attitudes exhibited by the Muslim community on many such issues as well as for the sharper role conflict situations that may be found in encounters with young Muslims. The Muslim attitudes can be better appreciated if the role of the family in Islam is properly understood.

Unlike the family structure of the host community, the family structure of the Muslims is not nuclear, but is extended to include well-defined rights and obligations which encompass the whole gamut of kinship relations. It is not uncommon in Muslim societies for several families to live together as one single and harmonious household, though this may not be prevalent in Britain. In-laws frequently live with their married offspring and enjoy a highly respected role within the group. A Muslim's home and food is always available to any of his relatives.

Muslim parents are enjoined in the Qur'ān to meet their family obligations scrupulously with kindness and justice. Similarly, the Qur'ān asks children to love and respect their parents; mothers in particular are presented as most worthy of respect, help and love. To their English neighbours, Muslim parents often appear very strict, but the deeply entrenched family loyalty and co-operative endeavour of the Islamic family is not based on negative parental sanctions; it is sustained by mutual trust and affection which emanate from the shared norms, values and beliefs of their religion – Islam; maintaining a network of satisfying human relations within the extended family group and creating a formidable social cohesion within the Muslim community as a whole.

Because of the particular nature of Islam as a total way of life and the role of the family in Islam, the younger generation of Muslims in Britain are often in a state of confusion and conflict in meeting religious and family obligations on the one hand, and gaining total acceptance within the host community in which they study and work on the other. As Muslims, they have the responsibility in the sight of God and the Muslim community as a whole, to preserve and develop the religion of Islam and transmit this faith to their children. As British citizens they are not unaware of their social and economic responsibilities to contribute to the general benefit of British society. To honour these often conflicting obligations, without compromise to their religion, imposes upon them many difficult adjustments and tensions. They deserve sympathy, understanding and respect, and need help from both Muslim adults and responsible authority within the host society.

In Britain, the problems of old people in society appear to be, to a great extent but not exclusively, the accepted responsibility of the State and a wide variety of voluntary social work agencies. In the Muslim community, it is taken for granted that grown-up children, married or single, will want to take care of their parents in the fullest sense of the word "care". Likewise, an old or retired Muslim knows that he can rely upon his children and can accept their help as part of the natural course of family life. Asked if he had any family, a 75-year old retired Muslim, on an extended tour of Europe and the Middle East, replied with confidence and pride, "Of course; seven – how do you think I could afford to travel otherwise?"

It is clear from the above discussion that the family bond in Islam entails mutual expectations of rights and obligations that are prescribed by religion, enforced by law, and observed by the group members. Accordingly, the family members share certain mutual commitments. These pertain to identity and provision, inheritance and counsel, affection and security for both the young and the aged, and maximization of effort to ensure the family continuity in peace.[1]

[1] Hammudah Abdulati, *The Family Structure in Islam*, A.T.P., Indianapolis, 1977.

2

Muslim Beliefs and Conduct

As already discussed, Islam, the religion of Muslims in Britain, is not merely a series of rites and rituals, nor is it a seventh day in the week event; "something" which should be kept in its proper place and not allowed to intrude upon the real job of earning a living and having a "good time". A Western writer sums up his understanding of Islam in these words: "It is a total and unified way of life, both religious and secular; it is a set of beliefs and a way of worship; it is a vast and integrated system of law; it is a culture and civilization; it is an economic system and a way of doing business; it is a polity and a method of governance; it is a special sort of society and a *way of running a family*; it prescribes for *inheritance* and *divorce, dress* and *etiquette, food* and *personal hygiene*. It is a spiritual and human totality, *this*-worldly and *other*-worldly."[1]

This may seem strange, but contrary to the popular notion, Islam lays great stress on the fact that it is not a new religion and that the Prophet Muḥammad (blessings of Allah and peace be upon him) did not bring a new faith. According to Muslim belief, he was only the last of a succession of Prophets which included, among many others, Abraham, Moses and Jesus, and renewed and reiterated what they had preached. He cannot be called the Founder of Islam, nor can Islam be called Mohammadanism; in fact to call Islam Mohammadanism would to a Muslim be both insulting and a reflection of total ignorance.

[1] Jansen, G.H., *Militant Islam*. London: Pan Books, 1979, p.17. (Emphasis is ours.)

Islamic life is based on two solid foundations – belief and action – and they are inseparable and complementary to each other. Beliefs must be rooted in the heart and are expressed in simple words. Desirable actions have been translated into a simple but comprehensive code of conduct. With Muslims, all individual, social and cultural expression emanates from their beliefs and code of conduct, and it is therefore necessary to throw some light on these before turning to specific aspects of Muslim life in Britain. While reading about Islamic beliefs and practices, many followers of other religions, especially Christians and Jews, may find an echo in their own hearts. This is not surprising in view of what has been explained above about Islam's claim that it is not a new faith.

BELIEFS

The fundamental beliefs that Islam teaches are the belief in One God; in all the Prophets of God, last of whom was the Prophet Muḥammad (blessings of Allah and peace be upon him); in all the Books of God, the last of them being the Qur'ān; and in the Day of Resurrection, the Day of Judgement and the life after death. Muslims also believe in the angels, as the servants of God who bring His message to the Prophets and obey and implement His commands.

God

Belief in the Oneness of God (or Allah, as Muslims prefer to call Him in Arabic) is the foundation of Islam, the bedrock of the Muslims' creed; an uncompromising and pure monotheism: God is One – Unique. The All-Powerful; the Sustainer and Nourisher of the entire world; in Whose hands are the life and death of all creatures. He is the Sovereign, the Law-Giver and the Administrator of the heavens and the earth; the Source of all guidance; the Just; the Forgiving and Merciful. He is with man wherever he is; the All-knowing, All-seeing, All-hearing. What distinguishes Islam's belief in God from that of other religions is, firstly, that it has no room for any compromise on the Oneness of God (*Tawḥīd*); and secondly, that it forms the basis and fount of all other Islamic beliefs, attitudes, practices and rules. A Muslim should worship or give his allegiance and loyalty to *none* apart from Him, or *in association* with Him, or *independent* of Him. He should have absolute trust in Him and love or fear none more than Him.

The belief in God permeates every walk of a Muslim's life and finds expression in every cultural or social practice, whether it be the etiquette of everyday life, the norms of human inter-relationships, the modes of eating and dressing, or even the slaughtering of animals. It is because of this that before any act, such as eating or sleeping or even driving a car, Muslims say *Bismillāh* (in the name of God) and in making promises and arrangements for the future, they say *Inshā' Allāh* (God willing). These simple invocations are a social expression of the Muslims' fundamental belief; in Islamic terms they convey a declaration of intent, gratitude and submission to the Divine Creator – an expression of faith.

Prophethood

God is the source of all true guidance for human life; man must submit to the Divine guidance as ultimate and final. Muslims believe that He has revealed His guidance to human beings chosen by Him for this purpose, called the Prophets. These Prophets came to all parts of the world, to all nations, at various times.

Adam was the first of the Prophets, and he and others – Abraham, Isaac, Jacob, Moses, Solomon, David, John and Jesus, to mention only a few – were all human beings chosen by God and were given the same message – "that God is One and His commands alone are to be obeyed". God refers to all these Prophets as Muslims because all of them followed the Right Path and were His true and faithful servants, to Whose will they submitted in all their deliberations and social actions.

Every Muslim is required, as an integral part of his faith, to believe and respect *all* the Prophets of God. Denial of one is the denial of all, and is enough to take one outside the fold of Islam. Muslims also recognize the tremendously influential and leading role the Prophets have played throughout history in communicating the message of God and demonstrating realistically the life which man, in strict accordance to nature, is recommended to follow.

Prophethood came to an end with Muḥammad (blessings of Allah and peace be upon him), whom God made the seal of all the Prophets and by whom the religion of Islam, a total way of life, was completed. It was to Muḥammad (blessings of Allah and peace be upon him) that the words of God were finally revealed, through the Angel Gabriel, over a period of twenty-three years, from the age of forty to sixty-three, when he died. The Qur'ān is the record of all these words exactly as conveyed and arranged by the Prophet himself.

The Prophet Muḥammad

The Prophet Muḥammad (blessings of Allah and peace be upon him) was born in Makka in the year 570 C.E. His father, 'Abd 'Allāh, died before Muḥammad's birth and his mother, Āminah, died when he was about six years old. His grandfather, 'Abd-al-Muṭṭalib, a prominent leader in Makka, then took charge of him. Upon the death of his grandfather, Muḥammad's guardianship passed to his uncle, Abū Ṭālib, who though never converted to Islam, showed great love and affection for his nephew until his death, when Muḥammad was fifty years old.

The Prophet's youth was similar to that of normal young Makkans – he fought in the battles, he joined the peace negotiations, and shared in the duties and rights of his society – except that he manifested from early years a revulsion to the worship of idols. Like other young men of Makka, he had to work; first as a shepherd and later as a businessman, through which he gained a reputation for being fair and honest, earning him the important titles of *al-Amīn* and *al-Ṣādiq* – the trustworthy and truthful.

At the age of twenty-five, he married a lady of forty, his first wife, Khadījah, a rich widow. They lived together for twenty-five years and had four daughters and two sons. Their sons died when very young and of the daughters who lived and married, only Fatimah had descendants, the Prophet's grandsons Hasan and Husain. Muḥammad was a devoted, loving father and was kind to children in general. In his twenty-five years of life with Khadījah, he was the ideal husband. Khadījah died when the Prophet was fifty, but it was during their last years together that Muḥammad received revelations from God.

Muḥammad (blessings of Allah and peace be upon him) was forty when he received the first revelations from God. He would frequently go to a cave on Mount Hirā just outside Makka, and there worship in solitude. It was while praying in the cave during the month of Ramaḍān that the angel Gabriel came to him with the first revelations from God. When he informed those close to him of his experiences, his sincerity was never doubted – his wife and his young cousin Ali who lived with him were among the first converts. While quietly preaching his faith in One God, he won further converts: his best friend, Abū Bakr, a wise, respected and rich merchant; later 'Uthmān and Ṭalḥah, equally important and well-to-do Makkans; and a number of poor citizens and slaves: they all joined the new faith that Muḥammad (blessings of Allah and peace be upon him) preached and became the nucleus on which the first Muslim community was based.

When the Prophet began to preach publicly, he met with considerable resistance to the new faith. During this period he was primarily concerned with the fundamentals of his faith: the Oneness of God, Prophethood, resurrection, the day of judgement, worship and the purification of the soul, all of which was alien and cut across the very fibre of Makkan society.

Makka was no longer a safe place for the Muslims. As a result of intense persecution faced by Muḥammad and his companions, they were forced to migrate to Madina, 400 kilometres away, where the people responded more readily to the new faith. At Madina the Prophet was able to set up the first city-state. Guided by revelation, he was able to implement the political and social structure of the new community, despite exposure to a war of annihilation.

Before his death in 632 C.E. and after years of bitter fighting between the Muslims of Madina and the idol worshippers of Makka, the Prophet (blessings of Allah and peace be upon him) was able to overpower his enemies and retake Makka in 630 C.E. This was one of the greatest days for the Muslims. The Prophet forgave the Makkans for all the years of sorrow and cruel scorn with which they had afflicted him and gave an amnesty to the whole population of Makka.

During his life, Muḥammad (blessings of Allah and peace be upon him) proved himself to possess a noble and spotless character, to be an absolute believer in one God, and thoroughly trustworthy in respect of his companionship, help and guidance. He was affectionate, kind and sympathetic to his compatriots; always considerate, truthful and sincere; perfectly faithful in respect of all trusts and promises. He kept himself aloof from gambling, drinking, vulgar wrangling, voluptuousness and all the vices rampant among the people of his age. He was always fair and honest in all his dealings; generous and obliging to his friends and benefactors. He walked humbly and thoughtfully in the midst of the arrogant. The Prophet's life, therefore, became the model and perfect example for all Muslims and for all times to come.

The Qur'ān: The Divine Source of Islam

All the prophets of God were given Divine Guidance through words, in the form of books. Muslims believe that the Old and New Testaments were originally Divine revelation. The Qur'ān is the latest and the last and enshrines all the basic teachings of the earlier revelations, whose original texts, according to the Muslim belief, were lost and are now found only in recensions and translations. Thus it is the first and fundamental source of guidance and is believed by Muslims all over the world to be final and ultimate, unchangeable in spite of changing human values and standards or human opinions and desires.

The Qur'ān is the foundation and the mainstay of Muslim life; it binds Muslims together, gives them a distinct identity and fashions their history and culture. It deals with all the important aspects of human life, the relationship between God and man, between man and man and between man and society, including ethics, jurisprudence, social justice, political principles, law, morality, trade and commerce.

The impact of the Book has not been confined to Muslims and their cultural accomplishments. It has influenced in many ways the mainstreams of human history and culture all over the world and has penetrated the thought and lifestyles of people belonging to different traditions. The Qur'ān, which means the "Reading", may not be the most widely printed and distributed book in the world, but it is certainly the most widely read and the most influential. Everywhere Muslims look to it for guidance and try to follow it.

Almost every Muslim home will be deeply concerned that the children learn to read the Qur'ān in Arabic. Indeed a Muslim child's first lesson is most likely to be the reading of the Qur'ān; hence the great efforts that the Muslims in Britain are making to establish evening and weekend schools to teach the Qur'ān. The Qur'ān is the main "liturgy" of Muslims; it is recited in prayers five times a day and on all other major and minor occasions. The recitation of the Qur'ān is an art in its own right; hundreds and thousands assemble to seek the joy of listening to it, while many are the proud owners of cassettes and records by famous reciters (called *Qārī*). So too is its calligraphy, where Muslims have excelled all other forms of art. Indeed, the Qur'ān exerts a tremendous impact on every cultural expression of the Muslims.

The Qur'ān is less in size than the New Testament. It consists of one hundred and fourteen chapters of very unequal length; those at the beginning being much longer than those at the end. The smallest unit is called a verse, there being 6,666 verses in the Qur'ān. The Qur'ān was revealed over a period of twenty-two years and five months. It is not arranged in chronological order, but its arrangement was dictated by the Prophet Muḥammad (blessings of Allah and peace be upon him) and its form, sequence and language has been preserved in the original shape as conveyed by the Prophet.

Since the Qur'ān is the word of God, Muslims have taken great pains to preserve it in Arabic – the language in which it was revealed. For centuries, they have even been averse to translating it into other languages. But there is no injunction in Islam prohibiting its translation and the first complete translation by Muslims was that made in 1737 in the Persian language by Shah Waliullah of Delhi.[1]

[1] The first complete Latin translation of the Qur'ān was made in 1143 by an Englishman, Robertus Retenensis, with the help of Hermannus Dalmata. (Cf. George Sale, *The Koran,* n.d., preface, vii). The first English translation of the Qur'ān was published in 1669 from London.

Muslims have also always been very particular, since the earliest times, about learning the Qur'ān by heart and committing it to memory in its entirety (called *ḥifẓ*). This has ensured that the Qur'ān has a long unbroken chain of transmission behind it. In fact, if today every copy of the Qur'ān were somehow lost, it would still be possible to rewrite the whole of the Qur'ān as it was given by the Prophet. Every year, during the month of fasting (Ramaḍān) the Qur'ān is recited in the night prayers. In every Mosque in Britain, a few children will always be found busy in committing it to memory.

Life after Death

Belief in life after death and the Day of Judgement is fundamental to Muslims who see this worldly life as part of the greater reality – the Hereafter. The life of this world would appear meaningless if it were not followed by an eternal existence in which reward and punishment are given to individuals in relation to their behaviour on earth. Paradise is the reward and Hell the punishment. On the Day of Judgement, each individual will be called to account for his or her conduct and rewarded accordingly.

This belief is crucial to Muslims and distinguishes their pattern of behaviour from that of others who have no firm conviction in this regard, and who are prone to modify their conduct in relation to immediate or foreseeable consequences within the confines of their limited perception of the segment of society of which they are part.

According to Islam, the present life is very brief and transitory and the life in the Hereafter will be eternal. The vivid description of what will happen on the Day of Judgement as also of Heaven and Hell has been given in the Qur'ān and other Islamic literature.

Man in Islam

According to Islam, man has been created as the representative (*Khalīfah*) of God on the earth. He has been given free will and moral sense. He is responsible for his actions. He carries no stigma of original sin. His natural urges and desires are not evil. They do not have to be repressed; only they should be controlled and fulfilled within the limits set by God. The rules and regulations for the conduct of human life have been clearly given in Islam which God has framed in keeping with human nature and bringing them in harmony with the forces of the Universe.

CONDUCT

Conduct is as important in Islam as faith. Both are almost invariably mentioned together in the Qur'ān. The faith in the heart must lead to good actions and morals in every aspect of life. In Islam, salvation lies in doing good deeds, and not merely in faith.

Worship

Worship in Islam, denoted by the Arabic word *'Ibādah*, is a much wider concept than in other religions. It can encompass a whole range of private devotions, social actions and human relations. Consciously and altruistically performed as acts of obedience to Islamic teaching, work, washing, bathing, cleaning, conversation, helping someone, study and so on, can be to the Muslim a form of worship if done with the sole intention of pleasing God and not merely to promote personal advantage, enhance status or put someone else under obligation to reciprocate etc.

The basic and formal structure of worship which enables a Muslim to transform his entire life into an act of worship is contained within the framework of the five pillars of Islam, which are as follows:

1 Declaration of Faith (*Shahādah*)
2 Prayer, five times daily (*Ṣalāh*)
3 Welfare Due, to the needy (*Zakāh*)
4 Fasting, during Ramaḍān (*Ṣawm*)
5 Pilgrimage, to Makka (*Ḥajj*)

Declaration of Faith: *Shahādah*

"I declare that there is no God but Allah, He is One and has no partner. And I also declare that Muḥammad (blessings of Allah and peace be upon him) is His servant and His Messenger."

These words will be on the lips of a Muslim as often as he can utter them – after rising from bed and before going to sleep, as he lives the day and before he dies. But for Muslims, this declaration goes beyond an habitual recitation; it is the essence of the frame of reference which guides their actions and determines their philosophy. In short, "There is no God but Allah, and Muḥammad is the Messenger of Allah" is not solely a prayer – it is the Muslims' plan of action.

Prayer, Five Times a Day: *Ṣalāh*

For Muslims, prayer is a regular and disciplined act of worship in which, mentally and physically, they humbly submit themselves to God, to praise Him, to glorify Him, to repent to Him and to seek mercy, forgiveness and guidance from Him. It takes the form of a series of rites which include standing, reciting the Qur'ān, bowing, prostrating and sitting.

All Muslims must pray, women and men, and in all circumstances of sickness, war and emergency etc. Children are also obliged to pray after the age of twelve, though they are encouraged to pray as soon as they can. During menstruation and in the post-natal period, women are exempt, as are both men and women who are not fully conscious or under the influence of drugs.

Prayer is obligatory five times a day at specifically stated periods: at dawn (*Fajr*), at midday (*Ẓuhr*), late afternoon (*'Aṣr*), after sunset (*Maghrib*) and late evening before going to bed (*'Ishā'*). Generally, Muslims are required to pray in congregation in the Mosque, where they assemble and stand in rows behind the *Imām*, the man whom they follow in all the rites of prayers. When this is not practically possible, they can pray more or less anywhere, wherever is clean and quiet, at home, at work, at school. As there is no hierarchy of priests in Islam, anyone of good moral character and well-versed in the Qur'ān can act as *Imām* to lead the prayers. The main congregational prayer held on Friday at midday in the Mosque is mandatory for men. Because of domestic responsibilities, the congregational prayer in the Mosque is optional for women, but they have every right to participate. During prayer, Muslims turn their faces towards Makka, wherever they may be. In Britain this direction, called *Qiblah*, is generally south-east.

Misdirected zeal, exhibitionism and fanaticism are alien to Islamic teaching, but Muslims are not allowed to miss prayers so long as it is possible not to do so. Although the prayers are compulsory and should be performed within specified periods, there is still sufficient flexibility to prevent real inconvenience. Prayers missed due to reasons beyond one's control can be made up later. According to some religious schools, in very special circumstances, and when travelling, the two afternoon and the two evening prayers can be performed together. There should certainly be no need for a Muslim bus driver (as was reported) to stop and park his bus, full of passengers, on the roadside while he prayed on the pavement, but if he does so he deserves sympathy and understanding, as would anyone else doing so under other genuine human needs.

Before praying all Muslims must perform a ritual act of purification which involves washing the hands, face, mouth, nose and arms (up to the elbow), lightly passing water over the head and washing the feet up to the ankles. After sexual intercourse, it is necessary for both husband and wife to take a complete bath before they can pray.

Welfare Due, to the Needy: *Zakāh*

Muslims believe that everything they possess has been given to them by God in trust; they are not the owners but merely the trustees. In Islam, all Muslims with sufficient means are obliged to give two-and-a-half percent of the value of their total wealth each year to the needy and for community projects. This is not a wealth tax: for the poor it is a right to assistance; for the better-off Muslims it is a means of purification and spiritual enrichment; and for the Islamic community it is a form of redistribution of income. Given with a sincere intention of perpetuating good and in gratitude to God for being in a position to do so, it is itself a form of worship. The collection of *Zakāh* is the responsibility of

Islam, but being an act of worship, it is not regarded as a burden, or like taxation, something to be evaded. In a country like Britain, the payment of *Zakāh* is left entirely to the conscience of the individual.

Fasting, in Ramaḍān: *(Ṣawm)*

Muslims are required to fast for one month each year – the month of Ramaḍān, the ninth month of the Muslim lunar calendar – abstaining from eating, drinking and sexual intercourse from dawn to sunset.

> "The month of Ramaḍān is the month when the Qur'ān was sent down as a guidance for mankind, and with clear expositions of guidance, and as a Standard. Let any of you who is at home during the month, fast in it; anyone who is ill or on a journey shall (set) a number of other days."
>
> "God wants things to be easy for you and does not want any hardship for you, so complete the period and magnify God because He has guided you, so that you may be grateful."
>
> (Qur'ān 2:185)

Fasting in the month of Ramaḍān is also one of the highest forms of *'ibādah* (worship) for Muslims. It is a test of moral character, an education and an opportunity to meditate. Whilst most people understand it to be merely an abstinence from eating, drinking and smoking (from dawn to sunset) during the 29/30 days of the sacred month of Ramaḍān, the fast, much more than a physical endurance test is, if performed with the sincere intention of pleasing God, a most fulfilling and enriching act of spiritual dedication. It should also lead to a special endeavour to abstain from all evil and sinful acts.

In paying welfare due (*Zakāh*) to the poor (which is normally done during Ramaḍān), Muslims have the opportunity of sharing their material possessions with the needy people, and in fasting they have the chance to share some of the anguish of hunger and poverty experienced by the distressed and destitute of the world. From this experience, they learn to be increasingly grateful and generous.

Fasting may create physical and economic hardships, but in Islam man has larger needs than the merely physical and economic. His spiritual growth and moral upliftment, so much dependent on self-control and self-discipline, is equally or, rather, more important. Whilst fasting is obligatory for all Muslims over twelve years of age, there are, in recognition of possible hardship, some exceptions: women during pregnancy, breast feeding and menstruation, and both men and women who are old, sick or infirm, and Muslims travelling. In cases of exception, the days can be made up at a later time or special payments equivalent to one day's food for each day of fasting made to help the poor.

The spiritual significance of the experience of Ramaḍān (*Ṣawm*) is illustrated below by an English Muslim's account of his first Ramaḍān:

> "Past my mid-forties and an Englishman accustomed to eating more than necessary and smoking like a chimney, I approached Ramaḍān with a fast growing apprehension; I had, as a new Muslim, succeeded in excluding pork from my menu, given up the dutch courage of excessive whisky and learned to control sexual desire outside of marriage, but to totally fast for 14 hours per day for 29 days seemed impossible on my past form of broken resolutions. I had ideas of going to Morocco to escape the temptations of England but it was not the Will of Allah. In answer to my prayers for help, I remained in England and taught a group of Muslim students. From them I learned to fast. From Allah I was given strength to fulfil both my spiritual and teaching obligations without great distress. On the contrary, at the permitted times for eating, after sunset and at dawn, Muslims make this a time for close and kindly relationship. My next Ramaḍān? I am apprehensive but I now know the energy and help to expect from worship – it is the Reward of Ramaḍān."

Pilgrimage, to Makka: ***Ḥajj***

> "Pilgrimage to the House is a duty mankind owes to God; for anyone who can find a way to do so."
>
> (Qur'ān 3:97)

Of the first four Pillars of Islam, the first two are daily duties, the second two are annual obligations; a pilgrimage to Makka is a once in a lifetime event of great magnitude and significance in the heart of every Muslim. To visit Makka is to visit the Ka'bah, the House of God, built by Abraham about four thousand years ago. *Ḥajj* is a command of Allah and for Muslims obeying this command, the sublime height of a true believer's worship of his Creator. Over two million Muslims make the pilgrimage to Makka each year and this great assembly of Muslims fervently demonstrate Islamic unity and solidarity, brotherhood and equality. Men or women, black or white, Arab or non-Arab, rich or poor, literate or illiterate, powerful or weak, ruler or ruled; together, *en masse*, wearing the same simple robe of unsewn white cloth; perform the same religious rites, standing and bowing, in one voice declaring – *Labbaik, Allāhumma Labbaik* (Doubly at Your service, O God, Doubly at Your service).

The rites of *Ḥajj* are performed from the 8th to the 13th of Dhu'l Ḥijja, the last month of the Islamic calendar. On the eighth day of this month, pilgrims go from Makka to Minā, a place about 8 kilometres from Makka and stay there all day. On the morning of the ninth day, the Day of *Ḥajj*, they go to 'Arafāt, a place about 15 kilometres from Makka and pray there all day long. The pilgrims leave 'Arafāt after sunset, spending the night at Muzdalafa, a place between 'Arafāt and Minā, and come back to Minā on the morning of the tenth day and stay in Minā till the evening of the twelfth day. During the pilgrimage, Muslims circle the Ka'bah seven times and walk between the two hills of Ṣafā and Marwā, situated near the Ka'bah.

A religious visit to Makka at any other time of the year is of great merit and is known as '*Umrah* or the lesser pilgrimage. Muslims visiting Saudi Arabia for business or other reasons, make it a point to perform '*Umrah* and visit the Mosque of the Prophet in Madina, where the tomb of the Prophet is also situated.

One of the features of *Ḥajj* (pilgrimage) is the sacrifice of animals made in commemoration of the Prophet Abraham (blessings of Allah and peace be upon him) who about four thousand years ago, willingly responded to his Lord's call and would have sacrificed his son Ishmael in submission to the

Will of God. In performing this sacrifice, Muslims demonstrate their own willingness to sacrifice their lives and their property for the sake of God and the religion of Islam.

Islamic Law – *The Sharīʻah*

Islamic Law, or the *Sharīʻah*, contains the code of conduct and behaviour in thought and action which Muslims are required to follow in their entire life. It embodies the Will of God and it is the duty of Muslims to do their utmost to live by it. It is the plan of action which the *Shahādah*, the first pillar, engenders, and for which the remaining four pillars train and discipline a Muslim.

Islamic Law is embodied in the Qur'ān and the life example of the Prophet Muḥammad, the *Sunnah*, and is the law revealed by God for Muslims. Islamic Law is not made by Muslims. In the light of contemporary situations it is interpreted by Muslim jurists but, once derived from the Qur'ān and the *Sunnah*, it can never, even by a comma, be changed. The Western mass media have tended to present a somewhat distorted and biased view of Islamic Law and associated it with particular Muslim countries in relation to singularly dramatic events. Its Divine nature and its universal application to all Muslims in the Islamic community is explained in the following excerpt from K.J. Murad's article, "*Sharīʻah*: The Way to God."[1]

> "The *Sharīʻah* is not merely a collection of 'do's' and 'don'ts', nor just a set of criminal laws prescribing punishments for certain crimes. Though it does contain both, its sweep is much broader and deeper, encompassing the totality of man's life. The *Sharīʻah* literally means a clear path. It is the path that man, in Islam, must walk as he toils and strives to reach his Creator.
>
> "It is the yearning deep within to seek the Lord and the Master that the *Sharīʻah* translates into steps, concrete and measured, on the pathways of life. The *Sharīʻah* is the fulfilment of the total man – inner and outer, individual and corporate – as he strives to live by the will of his One and only God.

[1] Published in a Saudi journal, "*Ahlan wa Sahlan*", No. 2, Vol. III, April-June 1979, pp. 28, 29.

"No part of man's life can be exempt from the need of divine guidance or free from the writ of divine sovereignty; that life is indivisible in submitting to its Lord. Hence the *Sharī'ah*'s claim to regulate every sphere of human life. There can be no distinction between the spiritual and the physical or the private and the public, and none can be excluded from the purview of the *Sharī'ah*. This does not mean that every single issue in human life has been settled for all time to come, but it does mean that wherever the *Sharī'ah* has laid down any principle or injunction, it cannot be evaded or ignored – it must be followed.

"The *Sharī'ah* consists of things which are (i) expressly prohibited (*ḥarām*), or (ii) expressly enjoined (*wājib*), or (iii) disliked but not prohibited (*makrūh*), or (iv) recommended but not enjoined (*mandūb*), or (v) simply permitted through silence (*mubāḥ*). Many do not realize that whatever is not prohibited is permitted and a major part of human life lies under *mubāḥ*, as the *Sharī'ah* prohibits only a few things.

"The *Sharī'ah* is also not equivalent only to laws enforceable through political authority, though they are an important and integral part of it. It overwhelmingly consists of morals, manners and regulations, from worship to statecraft, which depend for compliance entirely upon man's conscience."

Major Injunctions in Islam

"Say: Come, I will recite what your Lord has forbidden you:

1. Do not associate anything with Him;
2. And (show) kindness towards (your) parents.
3. Do not kill your children because of poverty; We shall provide for you as well as for them.
4. Do not indulge in shameful acts, be they open or secret.
5. Do not kill any person whom God has forbidden, except through (due process of) law.
   He has instructed you in this so that you may reason.
6. Do not approach an orphan's wealth before he comes of age, except to improve it.

7. Give full measure and weight in all fairness. We do not assign any person more than he can cope with.
8. Whenever you speak, be just; even though it concerns a close relative.
9. Fulfil God's covenant.
   Thus has He instructed you so that you may bear it in mind.
10. This is My Straight Road, so follow it and do not follow (other) paths which will separate you from His Path. Thus has He instructed you so that you may do your duty."

(Qur'ān 6:151–153)

The above verses give just one example of the general range of the beautiful teachings, injunctions and recommendations for good conduct and morality contained in the *Sharī'ah*. There are many other examples in the Qur'ān and in the teachings of the Prophet Muḥammad (blessings of Allah and peace be upon him) which it is not possible to include here.[1]

Major injunctions pertain to morals and ethics, but there are some specific prohibitions too: for example, eating any food derived from the pig, consuming alcohol, gambling, interest, fornication and adultery are specifically forbidden. At the individual level, these laws prevent Muslims from being mere slaves to their natural cravings and acquisitive instincts and protect them from unwholesome food. At the societal level, they protect the Islamic community from the social disruption caused by extra-marital sex, illegitimacy, marital disharmony and compulsive patterns of behaviour associated with drinking and gambling, and exploitation and avarice arising from interest. All of which, in a "permissive" society, contribute to psychological and emotional stress within the nucleus of society – the family. Even more important, obedience to these rules assures Muslims of an even greater reward than peaceful existence on earth; it guarantees them eternal happiness in the Hereafter. This is and has always been the main motivation and driving force

[1] See, for example, *The Qur'ān: Basic Teachings*, by T.B. Irving, K. Ahmad and M.M. Ahsan, Islamic Foundation, 1979.

behind the Muslim conduct of complying with the injunctions of the *Sharī'ah*.

Awareness of God

Following the articles of Faith, performing the acts of worship within the five pillars of Islam and obeying the commands of God, explicit in the *Sharī'ah*, imposes upon Muslims the necessity to be constantly aware of God. They must correct and modify their behaviour in accordance with Islamic teaching and acquire increasing knowledge for their application to life. Success in Islam is dependent upon the struggle each individual makes to overcome human weaknesses and instinctive desires. Some will falter, some may fall, but none will give up entirely.

Major Festivals in Islam

In Islam, there are two major festivals each year, *'Īd al-Fiṭr* and *'Īd al-Aḍḥā*, celebrated by Muslims as traditional feast days. In importance, but not in substance or symbolism, these festivals can be loosely equated with Christmas and Easter, celebrated by Christians.

Islamic festivals are not related to any particular season or person; they are both meant to celebrate the divine mercy shown in revelation and guidance and the human response in submission and sacrifice.

'Īd al-Fiṭr marks the end of the month of fasting, Ramaḍān, during which the revelation of the Qur'ān began. *'Īd al-Aḍḥā*, which falls on the day after the day of *Ḥajj* (Pilgrimage), celebrates the supreme example of sacrifice and submission exhibited by the Prophet Abraham (blessings of Allah and peace be upon him), as well as the declaration by God of the completion of the final divine revelation in the Qur'ān.

In Muslim countries, these festivals are celebrated, in both cases, mostly by a two-day national holiday. In Britain, they do not lose their importance to Muslims and are celebrated by the Muslim community with all the traditional joy and festivity characteristic of the celebrations throughout the Muslim world. British employers and educational authorities have become increasingly aware in this respect and the Muslims' right to be allowed at least one or two days leave from work, school or college to participate in the celebrations is being recognized.

'Īd al-Fiṭr

On this tremendously joyous festival, Muslims put on their new or best clothes and flock to the Mosques in the morning to pray in thanksgiving for the blessings they have received from God in the form of the Qur'ān and the keeping of the Fast. In prayers, both at home and in the Mosque, they also seek the mercy and forgiveness of God and ability to live by the Qur'ān. They also pay the *Ṣadaqah al-Fiṭr* (welfare due) for the poor.[1]

'Īd al-Fiṭr is both a community and a family celebration and on this day Muslims cook delicious meals, visit and embrace each other, and like any other festival, it is a special occasion for the children, who receive presents, sweets, new dresses and greetings. The air rings with greetings of *'Īd Mubārak* (Happy *'Īd*) and *As-salāmu 'Alaykum* (the peace of Allah be with you). To a Muslim, these greetings, and other expressions such as *Alḥamdulillāh* (Praise be to God), *Inshā' Allāh* (if God should so wish), *Bismillāh* (in the name of God) etc., are not just ritual verbalizations of the tongue, they are sincere responses of the heart expressing the Unity and Omnipotence of God; they arise from conviction.

Muslim festivals cannot really be transformed into commercial ventures like some other festivals. Extravagance, conspicuous consumption, prestige gifts, parties and discos are strongly discouraged in Islam, yet this creates no barrier to the genuine and spontaneous enjoyment of the delights and pleasures commonly associated with festival celebrations. *'Īd al-Fiṭr* is the Muslim community's assertion of unity and an Islamic expression of family solidarity, a time for prayer, thanksgiving and forgiving.

[1] *Ṣadaqah al-Fiṭr* is paid by the head of the family on behalf of all the members of the household (even for a newborn baby) and given to the poorer members of society to enable them to participate in the festival. In Britain the amount fixed for 1979 to be paid by each individual was 60p.

'ĪD AL-AḌḤĀ

The 'Īd al-Aḍḥā festival is yet another momentous event in the Islamic calendar and commemorates the time, 4,000 years ago, when the Prophet Abraham (blessings of Allah and peace be upon him) was, at the command of his Lord, willing to sacrifice his own son Ishmael as an act of obedience, devotion and submission to the Will of God. As a mercy upon the Prophet Abraham (blessings of Allah and peace be upon him) God accepted a lamb as a symbol of such devotion. Now, Muslims throughout the world symbolize their willingness to sacrifice their life and property in the name of God and for the cause of Islam. *'Īd al-Aḍḥā* coincides with the pilgrimage to Makka and it was on the day of pilgrimage, about fourteen centuries ago, that God declared the completion of the final divine revelations.

On this day, as well as on *'Īd al-Fiṭr*, Muslims put on their best clothes and attend congregational prayers in the morning. There is the same air of festivity and gaiety. Those who can afford to do so sacrifice an animal and share the meat among family, friends and the poor. In Muslim countries the streets are thronged with people, the air is incensed by the succulent smells of roasting meat and houses are crowded with people sharing the bounty of their Lord.

In Britain, too, Muslims celebrate *'Īd al-Aḍḥā* with the same Islamic balance of solemnity and spontaneous joy as in Muslim countries. They also sacrifice animals; an aspect which is not properly understood by the local community. Obviously it is not the very act of sacrifice and eating meat which is criticized, as there is no taboo against meat in Britain. The way of slaughtering is also something which has been practised by the Jews in this country for centuries. The Muslims are therefore unable to understand why the barrage of propaganda is directed against them each year on the occasion of *'Īd al-Aḍḥā*.

3

Muslim Practices and Attitudes

There are certain Muslim practices on which more information is required by people who are involved in various relationships with Muslims. These relate to aspects like food, dress, sex, marriage, family, public worship etc. Unfortunately, many popular opinions on these aspects are based on misunderstandings and myths thriving on ignorance, misinformation and half-truths.[1] It is therefore necessary not only to have full information on Muslim regulations and attitudes on these matters, but also to understand and respect norms and values which belong to a cultural milieu different from the Western, but in no way less civilized or inferior.

As many of these are equally relevant and important to the specific situations of home, school, work, hospital or prison, a general discussion would be helpful.

Basic Attitude

Islam develops a framework of life where *this*-worldly and *other*-worldly are fused and integrated into a whole. This world is not a place to run away from; it is a brief stay for being tested, purified and developed. Life must therefore be used fully. All good things on the earth are for man to use, but their use should be within limits prescribed by his Creator. Nothing created can be made unlawful without explicit authority from the Creator; there can be no taboos based on ignorance, superstition, traditions and customs. Islam also repeatedly urges that the needs and desires of the body are

[1] See Appendix, I.

not evil in themselves. All of them – food, drink, sleep and sex – should be satisfied; only when they are satisfied in violation of limits set by God do they become evil.

Food and Drink

According to Islam, all wholesome and good things are allowed to be used as food. As a general rule, every food is lawful unless it is declared unlawful. Islam provides guidance as to what food is unlawful (*ḥarām*).

All varieties of fish and all kinds of vegetables are lawful in Islam. It is only in the variety of meat that Islam discriminates between certain animals. Pig in all forms and carnivorous animals, whether slaughtered ritually or not, are specifically forbidden. It is likewise unlawful to eat even the fat or bones of the pig and carnivorous animals. Thus any food which contains lard will be unlawful, whether it be bread or ice cream. Moreover, an animal whose meat is otherwise lawful becomes unlawful if it is not killed ritually. Therefore, all animals that have died by natural causes or have been slaughtered contrary to Islamic law, e.g. killed by electric shock or sacrificed in a name other than that of God, or without taking the name of God, are unlawful.

According to Islamic law, the animal should be killed in such a way that blood flows out, usually by a very sharp knife penetrating the inner part of the animal's neck, and the name of God should be invoked upon it while it is being killed. Such meat is called *ḥalāl* and the Muslim community has established its own system of supplying *ḥalāl* meat through shops run by Muslims. The 'Kosher' meat of the Jews may also be eaten by Muslims, for the Jewish religion also prescribes slaughtering of animals in a similar way and mentioning the name of God over them.

Because of this regulation regarding ritual killing, the meat ordinarily found in the market, whether it is beef or sheep, cannot be consumed by Muslims. All other foods sold in the market, prepared or unprepared, which contain any meat or fat of animals which have not been slaughtered in the Islamic way are also unlawful for Muslims. A Muslim has to read the list of ingredients very carefully whenever he intends to buy any food in the market, but unfortunately in Britain giving information about ingredients is not legally binding as it is in the U.S. and on the continent. This restriction will take even some breads, ice creams, biscuits, soups etc. outside the list of what Muslims can eat in Britain.

With regard to drink, Islam prohibits all kinds of alcoholic drink, but permits all varieties of soft drink. Water is traditionally used at meals. The law relating to alcohol is very strict and there are no exceptions. If the slightest amount of alcohol is used in the preparation of food, e.g. game soup, sherry trifle, plum pudding and Christmas or wedding cakes, etc. they become unlawful (*ḥarām*) for Muslims to consume.

Dress

Islam has not prescribed any particular dress. It has given broad outlines and enjoined Muslims to cover their bodies properly and decently. The minimum part of the body that should necessarily be covered for a man is from his navel to his knees and for a woman from her head to her feet, leaving only the face and hands. As to the shape of the garment, its colour and design etc., no particular instructions have been given. They have been left to the requirements and choice of the individual. Islam enjoins both men and women to observe these rules of modesty and not to be ostentatious in their dress and behaviour.

Sex and Family

Islam inculcates a very healthy and wholesome attitude towards sex. It is recognized as a genuine need of the bodily life which should be enjoyed and satisfied properly. It is a gift from God and should be enjoyed in a spirit of gratitude and thankfulness.

The only limit which Islam places is that the bond of marriage must be tied before enjoying the pleasures of sex. For these pleasures are the rewards for the heavy responsibilities of rearing a family; they lighten the burden and cement the tenuous relations. To seek sex outside the bond of marriage is a sin; therefore to seek it within the limits set by God is an act of worship:

> "Marriage is the only foundation of family; and family is the foundation of society. If sex with or without marriage

was equally legitimate or easily available, the most important and sacred institution of marriage would be gradually destroyed."[1]

Hence the various Islamic regulations and Muslim attitudes regarding dress, intermingling of the sexes, co-education, mixed swimming, dating, polygamy etc. For Muslims believe that prevention is better than cure. Anything which is not essential for the individual or society and which may lead to inducement to sex outside the bond of marriage is not permitted in Islam.

Public Facilities for Worship

Islam is distinguished from other religions in that it prescribes ritual prayers five times a day, in addition to the weekly congregation on Friday noon. This naturally leads to worship in public places, in schools, places of work, hospitals etc. and consequent need for proper facilities for ablution and prayers. Those who are not used to such a rigorous routine of prayers or accustomed to the Muslim practices, feel inconvenience and difficulty in adjusting to the Muslim schedule or in providing the required facilities. The prayer is a spiritual punctuation of the material day; without the opportunity for prayer, a true believer experiences a feeling of void and loss. To provide prayer facilities in schools, colleges, work places, hotels and community centres etc. is not really difficult in relation to either time, situation or space.

TIME

Winter: The winter months, after the end of British Summertime, do bring the midday (*Ẓuhr*), the afternoon (*'Aṣr*) and the after-sunset (*Maghrib*) prayers very close together, but there is quite a degree of flexibility in which these prayers, (of about ten minutes duration) can be given. The midday prayer can be timed at schools and work places to coincide with the lunch break between 12 noon and 1.00 p.m.; the afternoon prayer between 2.30 p.m. and 3.30 p.m.

[1] *Sharia: The Way of Justice*, by K. J. Murad in "Ahlan wa Sahlan," Vol. III, No. 3, July 1979.

and the after-sunset prayer between 4.00 p.m. and 5.00 p.m. The morning prayer can, in most cases, be said at home from dawn to about 7.30 a.m. and the night prayer (which would only affect shift workers and hostel residents) can be said any time till dawn of the following day, though before midnight is strongly recommended.

All Muslims will in fact have a detailed timetable and the above are just the suggested times at which all Muslims could be brought together to pray. With co-ordination from all departments or classes and the Muslims concerned, an agreed timetable, within the limits of the permitted flexibility, could easily be arranged.

Summer: This provides little real difficulty as the time gaps between each prayer are quite long; in schools and colleges the midday (*Ẓuhr*) prayer is the only one that needs to be arranged and this can be between 1.00 p.m. and 4.00 p.m., as there is usually sufficient time to return home before the late afternoon prayer (*'Aṣr*). At work, arrangements are certainly easier in summer than in winter. The morning prayer (except for night workers) can be said at home, the midday prayer as for schools, between 1.00 p.m. and 4.00 p.m., and the afternoon prayer up to about 30 minutes before sunset. The total time involved in winter is about 35 minutes per day; in summer it is considerably less.

Situation, Space and Sanitation

Any clean, quiet and vacant room can be used; ideally a room set aside for the purpose would be preferable, but it is certainly not essential. A vacant classroom, conference room or even store room can be used. At work, Muslims would no doubt appreciate a room set aside for them and would be willing to contribute towards the cost of maintenance and decoration.

The Friday Congregational Prayer (*Ṣalāt al-Jum'ah*)

All Muslim males over twelve years of age are obliged to attend the Mosque for the Friday prayer. When it is absolutely impossible to attend the Mosque because of distance, the

Muslims concerned should make every effort to establish Friday prayer within the educational or industrial establishment. The time involved in the actual prayer is less than an hour.

However, every effort should be made to attend the Mosque and the time involved for this, accounting for travelling and lunch, is about 1½ to 2 hours, and therefore the employers should co-operate with their Muslim employees by extending their lunch hour by 30 minutes or an hour to allow them to attend the Friday prayer. In Islam, unlike Christianity and Judaism, there is no Sabbath day as such, and Friday for Muslims in a foreign country (in which they have weekends) is not a full day's holiday; Muslims are required to leave trade and sport for the Congregational prayer, then continue with business and permitted pleasures. Employers and schools are strongly urged to help Muslims to meet this most important religious obligation. Muslims in return are usually willing to make up lost working time and study hours in the evenings and at weekends.

Facilities For Ablution For Prayer

Whatever kind of space is allocated for the Muslims' prayer, it is essential that they have access to running water for ablution (*wuḍū'*) before prayer. The strict requirements for washing (*wuḍū'*) do sometimes cause tension and friction; indigenous workers and European students often experience a feeling of disgust at seeing feet being washed and noses cleaned in the washbasin. The tension and ill-feeling generated on this and the sensitive issue of toilets where water is used to clean the private parts, would appear to justify separate washing and toilet facilities for Muslims without in any way seeming to condone segregationist policies in industry or schools. A simple room divider could very easily solve the problem to the mutual satisfaction of both groups involved. Ideally, foot baths could be made available. And in ratio to the number of Muslims involved, a given number of "stand up toilets" could be installed in which running water was available for the Muslims to clean themselves without causing distress to others by leaving water on the floor, which in any case should be cleared up before leaving. Co-operation is a two-way activity and Muslims must come half-way at least to solving their own problems, without, of course, compromising their religion.

4

The Muslim Child at School

Having discussed briefly the various aspects of Muslim belief, conduct and practice, we would now like to look at specific areas where Muslims need understanding in expressing and observing their religious duties. The areas of greatest concern are the Muslim child at school, Muslims in employment, Muslims in medical care and Muslims in penal institutions.

The needs of the Muslim child at school are the most important and there are some major issues which have caused concern amongst parents and community leaders. These are role conflicts, language, co-education, religious education in school, sex education, dress and food.

Language

The Muslim child in Britain is likely to speak his native language (Urdu, Bengali, Punjabi or Gujarati in most cases) at home, Arabic in prayers and English in school. In the formative years of socialization this may seem to impose psychological tensions on the pupil and create a confusion in communication and comprehension, further aggravated by a hotch-potch of muddled notions created by different religious and cultural symbols like Father Christmas, Easter, Jesus, Muḥammad (blessings of Allah and peace be upon them), God and Allah etc. However, given understanding by teachers and with the co-operation of the Mosques, the child's own adjustive mechanisms will be able to cope with the experience – probably turning a linguistic handicap into a social asset in later life. Children learn languages easily and naturally and, much more than parents and teachers often realize, are very resourceful and resilient and adjust to new situations with greater ease than adults.

However, it is important that the child is not discouraged from coping with these three languages. Arabic is the language of Islam which he must use in prayers and other religious rites. It preserves the Divine revelation in original form and imparts homogeneity and cohesion to the Muslim community, otherwise composed of so diverse ethnic and linguistic backgrounds. Without Arabic the inner message of the Qur'ān also remains hidden, regardless of the extent to which the pupil may read it in English translation. The language of his parents is the means by which the child learns to identify with his/her culture (in the same way as the Welsh preserve the cultural heritage of Wales through the Welsh language and French Canadians in Canada etc., etc.). English is the essential tool by which the child learns to live in his new home, Britain, and to adjust to a second culture and communicate within the framework of its social, educational and economic institutions. In social and educational terms, therefore, it is essential that the Muslim child is given the opportunity, both in and out of school, to learn these three languages and adjust to the often conflicting value systems they communicate.

Role Conflict

A Muslim child faces a very distressing conflict situation with respect to the many and varied roles he is required to play. Any child in modern society faces this problem to some extent as he passes through various socializing agencies, each communicating a different message. But for a Muslim child the situation is much more acute. The parents, with their Islamic, ethnic and village background; the family, the peer group within and outside the home; the mass media; the school environment; the teacher; the text book; and society in general – all combine together to put upon him very confusing and conflicting demands.

What he therefore needs is a very high degree of sympathy and understanding from his home and his school. Given moral support from the family, guidance from the Mosque and religious tolerance and respect from teachers and community workers, the young Muslim can learn to fulfil the rights and obligations incumbent upon his/her many social roles in a Muslim environment and within the British society without the slightest necessity for religious compromise.

Co-education

Another major issue confronting Muslim parents living in Britain is co-educational schooling of their children, which goes against the teachings of Islam. The mixing of the sexes in and out of the adolescent stage is contrary to the ethos of Islamic teachings. The great issues are the danger of developing relationships in co-educational schools leading to sexual permissiveness and the degradation of morals.

The Muslim desire for single-sex education should not be underestimated, as it is based on very important and clear Islamic injunctions. It should be recognized that in Britain there is a well-meaning and silent section even of non-Muslim parents who would, surely, favour a single-sex school education for their children if there was a free choice and provision of such schools. As far as Muslim parents are concerned, they would all prefer such an arrangement. It is not infrequent to hear of cases of girls being sent back to their country of origin or kept at home in England because of the lack of facilities for single-sex education.[1] Given the multi-style system of schooling in this country and growing shift towards free parental choice, the one acceptable solution will be to continue the provision of single-sex schools within the maintained school system.

Religious Education

All children have the *right*[2] to be taught the religious belief and moral code of their parents, be they Christians, Jews, Hindus, Sikhs, Buddhists or Muslims, because it is upon a shared belief that family stability depends and from a religious commitment that a system of lasting norms, values and morality emerges.

1 See, "Muslim girls may be sent home to study" by John Fairhall in the *Guardian*. Wednesday, November 21, 1979.
2 Vide Education Act 1944 and the Children Act 1989.

In a world torn by revolution and aggression, it is reassuring to note that in Britain there is a high degree of religious tolerance and respect expressed at both official and community level. It is this natural tolerance and respect which has enabled Christians and Jews, Catholics and Protestants, Methodists and Jehovah Witnesses peacefully to co-exist over a period of many years. The Muslim community, the largest minority, is relatively new to Britain and the problems which they face do not stem from religious antagonism, or, generally speaking, racism, but rather from cultural differences and the aura of mystery and misconception associated with Islam. The basic problem is one of communication – a two-way communication between Muslims and the local community. One of the advantages of bringing Islamic instruction into the schools would be to bring Islam into the open and to let people see Muslims as they are and thus erase the fantasy images projected on T.V. and in the press.

Religious and moral instruction for the Muslim is particularly essential because Islam, unlike other religions, is a living faith which demands adherence in conduct and behaviour. There is no division in Islam between the secular and the sacred. To practise Islam would not be possible without knowledge.

Important also is the fact that believing and practising Muslims should give religious and moral education to Muslims. If adequate arrangements for religious teaching are not made at school level, separate schools will spring up, as is happening now, placing more strain on Muslim students.

Sex Education

Directly related to the necessity to provide regular Islamic instruction to Muslim students is the controversial issue of allowing Muslims to attend classes scheduled as sex education. In fact, the way sex education is imparted goes against the teachings of Islam. Islam puts great emphasis on modesty and morality, which are badly offended by the mode and contents of prevalent sex education. Islam does not allow any graphic illustration of sexual organs and sex play. This is disgusting to a Muslim's sense of decency.

Islam, of course, does not stand for ignorance and has its

own method of sex education. But this is entirely different from what is practised as sex education in schools today. Islam teaches from the very beginning how to handle the sex organs when one is in the toilet, what to do if there is ejaculation, how girls should behave if their monthly cycles begin, etc.[1]

Muslim parents argue that the sex education as taught in the West will lead to moral degradation of their children and will certainly have a bad effect on their overall training and upbringing. This is why at a recent Muslim Teachers' Association Conference for both parents and teachers, the general view of the parents was solidly against sex education in schools.[2]

Dress

School uniform, especially for girls, is one of the sensitive issues about which Muslim parents feel very strongly as in some cases it does not conform to the Islamic regulations. They are not opposed to the idea of school uniform as such, or any particular type of dress, but express great anxiety at the possibility of their daughters breaking Islamic laws pertaining to dress. Total covering of the body is so basic to Islamic teaching and practice that Muslim parents rightly argue that their daughters should observe these standards from the very beginning. There have been incidents in which Muslim parents have fought quite vehemently over the issue of school uniform. As an alternative solution, they have shown great willingness to acquire *shalwār* (Asian-style trousers), maxi-skirts and slacks of the same colour and texture as the uniform blazer and coats, to which they have no objection. These alternatives to the uniform skirt are generally considered to be acceptable to Muslims and an increasing number of headmistresses and headmasters have also accepted them as suitable alternatives and, indeed, in many cases shown a

1 See *Sex Education, the Muslim Perspective,* published by the Muslim Educational Trust.

2 Conference held at the Islamic Cultural Centre, London, April 1979. Speaking in a general discussion on sex education for children, a Muslim parent stated: "It is in the nature of men and women to know what to do when the right time is blessed by marriage – for a Muslim, explicit guidance on morality, marital relationships, love and affection are clear in the Qur'ān.

great deal of sympathy and understanding when dealing with the skirt/trouser controversy.

Physical Training and Sport

Connected with dress is the question of physical training of boys and girls. It has been encouraged in Islam, and Muslim parents are anxious to see their children receive it. But the main difficulty which worries Muslim parents, and indeed contravenes Islamic regulations, is (a) mixed P.T. of boys and girls and (b) the use of costumes which expose some delicate part of the body which is required to be covered. If these two difficulties regarding mixed classes and dress are resolved, Muslim children and students can take part in swimming, school games and physical training programmes.

According to Islamic teachings, boys and girls should be separated at about the age of ten. In the matter of dress, the following rules can be easily observed.

Boys: Normal type shorts of about boxer length worn over underbriefs, or in many cases, track suit trousers may be suitable. 'T' shirts/vests are also recommended for activities other than swimming, rather than a nude torso. Shorts for P.T. and swimming should be loose fitting and fit above the line of the navel.

Girls: Under no circumstances must any part of the body except the face be exposed. Track suits or tight trousers, or in some cases leotards, may be worn along with a 'sweat' shirt or 'T' shirt, under which a normal vest or bra is recommended if this does not impose physical constraints on movement. For swimming, leotards and tops are convenient and are not dissimilar to, but much lighter than the kit skin divers' wear.

After-sport Baths and Showers: Muslim boys should not be asked to take communal showers without wearing appropriate covering of their private parts and likewise, girls in the female shower rooms must certainly not go around without proper covering.

Mixed Bathing: Muslims, male or female, in schools or at

Youth/Sports Centres or public swimming baths etc., cannot take part in mixed bathing.

Fasting in the Month of Ramaḍān

Children above the age of twelve are obliged to fast during the month of Ramaḍān. Therefore it is likely that most of the older pupils in schools may fast. It may not be obligatory for them all, but in so doing, they will receive encouragement from older members of the family and will feel proud that they are learning to observe their religious duties and adopting the customs of adult Muslims. Younger children may pretend to others that they too are fasting because they are strongly motivated to express public identification with their religious group.

Children who are fasting may feel weak and tired during the day, especially in the afternoon. Strenuous physical exercise may make them feel worse. They should not be asked to drink milk or eat anything during school hours. Those who normally stay for school lunches will probably want to go home. If this is inconvenient for the parents, it should be possible for children to remain in school during the lunch hour. Those children who go swimming may be concerned about swallowing water – strictly speaking this would be breaking the fast – so they will spit it out.

Teachers should avoid giving the impression that fasting is "a nuisance, disruptive to school routine and work", but should view it as something positive. They must accept that a child's attitudes, behaviour and performance may in some cases be affected, but that these changes are purely temporary. They should acknowledge their acceptance of fasting by showing interest and asking questions about fasting routines. They should accept that Britain is a multi-religious and multicultural society; tolerance and respect should be given to the other's faith and culture.

Food and Drink

The Islamic regulations regarding food and drink have already been discussed in Chapter 3. To provide *ḥalāl* meat to Muslim pupils and students should not really present any great difficulty[1] as there are many sources of supply within the Muslim community. Arrangements for a regular supply of *ḥalāl* meat could be made with the co-operation of one of the Muslims in the community.

As ingredients are also vital, every effort should be made to cook food either in vegetable oil or in butter or vegetable margarine. Animal fat should never be used. However, there is no need for separate utensils if washed ones are used when preparing Muslim food and they are not mixed with non-*ḥalāl* food during the preparation of food. If, for any reason, *ḥalāl* meat is not available on a certain day, alternative arrangements for fish, eggs and vegetables should be made. Under no circumstances should a Muslim pupil be obliged to eat ordinary non-Kosher meat or any food which has been prepared in lard or other animal fat. This is the reason, as explained earlier, that Muslims are very careful when buying food from the market. They will not buy bread, biscuits, crisps, ice-cream, etc. until they are sure of the purity of the ingredients involved.

Drinking alcohol is totally prohibited in Islam, but this aspect usually does not present any problem in school. However, it must be realized that even a very cold morning, a nasty shock, anxiety condition or an accident, etc., cannot provide the Muslim with an excuse to take a 'nip' of brandy. A cup of black tea or coffee with plenty of sugar, however, would be appreciated in these circumstances.

Recommendations

Schools, colleges, universities and youth clubs in co-operation with parents, Mosques and organizations within the Muslim community could achieve a great deal at both local and national level once basic principles and agreed objectives were formulated. Below are a few suggestions, some of which are already successfully functioning in various parts of Britain.

[1] It is heartening to note that the Inner London Education Authority has recently issued a directive to its 1,100 schools to observe Hindu and Muslim dietary regulations in the preparation of school meals. See, "Taboo on School Food" in the *Daily Telegraph*, Saturday, October 6, 1979.

1. Muslim teachers in schools with a high percentage of Muslim pupils could be asked to volunteer to act as religious instruction co-ordinators and welfare officers/consultants on problems which appear to be aided by an empirical knowledge of Islam. It must be noted that all Muslims have a duty to guard, protect and encourage the religious interests of fellow Muslims. In particular, the young Muslim teachers are not likely to decline a request genuinely aimed at improving the educational/social facilities of their brothers and sisters in Islam.

2. Time and classrooms allocated for religious instruction of Muslim pupils by Muslim teachers in schools.

3. Provision of a prayer room, adjacent to washing facilities for congregational worship.

4. Invitations to *Imāms* and Islamic scholars to visit and give talks in the school.

5. In social studies and in general religious studies, allowing Muslims, rather than non-Muslims, to present Islam to the school generally, with the promotion of religious tolerance and understanding in view.

6. Arrangements for non-Muslim pupils to visit the Mosques.

7. Enlisting the support of a Muslim teacher to be responsible for encouraging Muslim parents to attend parent-teacher meetings, and having interpreters in Asian languages available to assist parents in discussing the educational programme and problems of their pupils.

8. Inviting *Imāms* and Muslim scholars to accept positions and take an active part on school, college and youth centre management committees, especially committees like SACRE.

9. Allowing Muslim children to withdraw from collective worship and morning assemblies, where they are Christian-orientated.

10. Allowing Muslim boys and girls to be absent from sex education classes.

11. In institutions and organizations with a high percentage of Muslims, it may not be economically unfeasible to employ a full or part-time cook and have a separate cooking unit.

12. The preparation of a wide range of vegetarian dishes – salads, cheese and mushroom omelettes, fish, rice, macaroni, spaghetti and boiled eggs etc.

13. In schools, it is particularly important that children are not placed in circumstances in which they are forced either to eat unlawful food or go hungry.

14. In cookery classes, Muslim pupils must not be allowed to prepare meals from pork or other unlawful ingredients.

Whilst it is appreciated that the implementation of these recommendations may occasion some initial inconvenience and slight reorganization, we firmly believe that the advantages gained by removing sources of conflict and tension make the effort worthwhile.

5

Muslims in Employment

The Muslim employee, speaking generally (and not discounting the many educated Muslims employed in the professions, civil service, management, skilled trades and self-employed in business) is likely to have been brought up in a rural environment, be very aware of his identity and obligations as a Muslim and draw his strength from his Islamic background. He is, however, also likely to have a serious communication problem; his knowledge of the English language may be inadequate to communicate the full range of his feelings, ideas and requirements and incapable of fully comprehending the requirements, ideas, structure and rationale of the social and economic institutions of a non-Muslim industrial culture. In all probability, he will have had even less education and educational opportunity than his children educated here and, as a natural reaction to previous and existing racial discrimination and prejudice in this country, be defensive, sometimes aggressive and inwardly cautious, though always sincerely trying to be friendly in social relationships with non-Muslims. Muslims in Britain may show a great national pride and an ardent desire to preserve their Islamic identity. On closer analysis one may even discern, among a minority, provincial attitudes and, as among English workers, regional and political rivalries thriving. These real and uncontrived handicaps to social integration with the host society present themselves at two distinct levels:

(a) In the community, they create difficulty in relation to employment, industrial education and training, trade union membership, legal responsibilities under British law, e.g. education and marriage law (as distinct from Islamic law to which they are definitely committed), commercial transactions, housing and welfare, health and social services.

(b) In the family, in relation to their children who become more socially adaptable under social pressures, the Muslim worker's relative attachment to his cultural norms creates a further dimension to the generation gap, and stable relationships within the family (which are basic to good Islamic practice) are threatened by communication problems at home and "strange" attitudes to life which the children bring from outside.

The Muslim worker is usually Islamically orientated, family centred and economically motivated. He is earnestly concerned to provide an increasingly higher standard of life and social opportunity for his immediate family in Britain and to meet his social and economic obligations to relatives in other cities of Britain and country of origin. At the same time, he strives to practise Islam in an environment which provides him with a wide range of temptations, e.g. alcohol, gambling, fornication, adultery, etc., which are more accessible than at home. Sociological evidence indicates that though disposed to follow his religion, identify with his culture and exist self-sufficiently within the Muslim community, the Muslim worker does genuinely try in industrial, educational and social institutions to comply with the law, meet constructive demands made upon him and form friendly relations with workmates, classmates, shopkeepers and the man in the street.

The Qur'ān explicitly forbids Muslims to drink alcohol, eat anything produced from the pig, to gamble and to engage in any form of usury. To a British worker, brought up in Western society, these religious laws may appear a harsh limitation on the freedom of man. To a convinced Muslim worker, on the other hand, drinking alcohol, eating pork, backing horses and money lending or interest are equally alien. A non-Muslim may quite lightheartedly and without any malice invite a Muslim workmate to have a pint of beer or place a bet on a horse. To the Muslim, this social invitation is in fact a provocation to break the laws of his religion and bring to him unhappiness in this world and punishment in the next.

Islam forbids all forms of pre-marital and extra-marital sexual relations. The Muslim worker is strengthened in his resolve to comply with the Islamic injunctions by a steadfast belief that sex, and the undisputed pleasures it brings, is lawful only by a contract of marriage based on love, commitment and respect and mainly motivated by a desire on the part of the man and wife to bring up a family of strictly practising Muslim children. However, in a society in which attitudes to sexual behaviour are by contrast described as permissive, these restrictions on sexual satisfaction may invite disbelief and even ridicule from non-Muslim workmates. To the Muslim worker they certainly do create a need for a greater personal struggle over human frailty but for the real believer, the realization of Islam is dependent on his sincerity of intention and his willingness to resist these temptations.

In their attempts to live by Islam, Muslim workers simply require their non-Muslim workmates, be they Christians, Jews, agnostics or atheists to respect their right to follow the religion of Islam, and are usually very grateful for any help they receive from Trade Unions, management or workmates in this respect.

There are some Muslim workers who fail to obey the laws of their religion and do drink and consort with women outside of marriage, but it is a fallacy to believe that, having fallen victim to his own weakness, the Muslim worker is becoming "absorbed" into the host community. On the contrary, he will become, to some extent, alienated from the Muslim community and by his very nature unable to reject or deny his religion, he is likely to develop a tremendous sense of guilt and irrationally begin to resent the society in which he "fell" and become a problem to both Muslim and non-Muslim workers. A worker with a guilt complex does not make an efficient contribution to the organizational objectives of the firm.

It is in the interests of industrial establishments and the community as a whole to encourage Muslims to follow their religion. This can be done by according respect to Islam and providing really good facilities for the Muslim workers to observe religious duties. Paradoxically, to encourage their separate religious identity can, in the long run, contribute to their efficiency as workers and their ability to relate to the indigenous workers generally. Islam is the powerhouse of the Muslim worker's strength and motivation, his guidance, his value-system and his refuge. If he loses or neglects it, he becomes a disintegrated personality and a belligerent worker.

The main areas where the Muslim employee finds difficulty in observing religious duties may be identified as follows:

1. Facilities for the daily prayer;
2. Facilities for fasting in the month of Ramaḍān;
3. Leave during the two annual festivals;
4. Muslim food.

Prayer Facilities

The extent of facilities required for daily prayers, Friday prayers and ablution (*wuḍū'*) have been discussed earlier in Chapter 3 and are equally applicable to work situations. It should not be difficult for any employer to find ways and means to provide these facilities. What should be recognized is that any daily prayer hardly requires more than ten minutes, and this much time is made available for even going to washrooms or having tea or chatting with a friend. Similarly, a Muslim does not have to go to a Mosque; he can very well pray in the same place as where he is working.

Working Hours during Fasting (Ramaḍān)

As fasting is obligatory for all Muslims above the age of twelve, it is likely that Muslims at work will be fasting during the month of Ramaḍān. Fasting starts at dawn and ends at sunset and between these hours food, drink, smoking are not allowed. Usually a family will wake before dawn to have a meal (*suḥūr*) marking the beginning of the fast, so as to provide some nourishment for the rest of the day.

The fast may put some extra strain on the Muslim worker, especially in summer, when daylight is of 17–18 hours duration. He will do his best to do his job satisfactorily as he is enjoined by Islam to do. Employers should avoid giving the impression that fasting is a nuisance and disruptive to the working routine, but should view it as something positive to every Muslim.

In view of the fact that Muslims will not require breaks for tea and lunch, except for a few minutes for the midday prayer, employers could consider the possibility of shortening as well as adjusting the working hours according to mutual convenience. For the night shift workers, it will be helpful if self-catering facilities are provided for their early morning meal (*Suḥūr*). These steps will undoubtedly help the Muslim worker in completing the fast without difficulty and will foster better industrial relations.

Leave during the Two Annual Festivals

As explained earlier in Chapter 2, the two major festivals of Islam are (a) *'Īd al-Fiṭr* at the end of the month of Ramaḍān and (b) *'Īd al-Aḍḥā* at the end of *Ḥajj*, two months and ten days after *'Īd al-Fiṭr*. In Britain, Muslims celebrate both festivals with all the traditional joy and festivity. On both these occasions, the male members of the family attend the Mosque or a specific hall which the community hires for this purpose. The prayer is held in the morning usually between 9.00 a.m. and 11.00 a.m. and the duration of the prayer is about half an hour. After the prayer, Muslims greet and embrace each other and during the course of the day they visit each other at home. They will therefore require at least one day off on both festivals to celebrate the occasion in a proper manner.

Since the Islamic calendar is based on the lunar system, the dates of these festivals are not fixed and vary from year to year. Moreover, because the lunar dates depend upon the sighting of the new moon, Muslim workers may not be aware of the exact date of these festivals in any particular year much in advance. However, the responsibility of informing about the dates rests on Muslim workers and community leaders, who should inform employers of the festival dates as soon as possible. This will enable the management to make alternative arrangements, so that the Muslim workers can participate in the joyous occasions that these festivals bring. It is hoped that the employers will patiently bear with any uncertainties and inconveniences.

Muslim Food

As mentioned previously,[1] Muslim dietary regulations are markedly different from those of non-Muslims. Bacon and other foods produced from the pig are strictly forbidden to a Muslim. Beef, chicken and lamb are forbidden if not slaughtered according to Islamic law as mentioned earlier. In some cases, a Muslim may restrict himself to a diet of egg, fish, cheese and vegetarian dishes; however, this may not be for prolonged periods. It is recommended that employment institutions provide the necessary facilities for Muslim food, since this does not impose upon the catering staff any greater inconvenience than the preparation of special diets required by other employees such as Jews and diabetics etc. It would also be helpful if provision is made for self-catering units in which Muslims can warm up previously prepared food.

[1] See, Chapter 3. pp. 36, 37; see also Chapter 4, section 'Food and Drink', pp. 49, 50.

6

Muslims in Medical Care

A visit to the local doctor, a consultation with a specialist, or a short stay in hospital may create anxiety even in an ordinary patient. The impact on a Muslim who is anxious not to violate any Islamic injunction can be quite disturbing. Modesty is an obligation in Islam; consequently the Muslim, male or female, is extremely shy about being naked and very reluctant to expose private parts (*'awrah*), though it is permissible in Islam on medical grounds.

Not only are female patients disinclined to be examined by male doctors, male patients are equally unwilling to consult a female doctor. For Westerners, used to a more "broadminded" outlook this may seem very trivial and "narrow-minded". However, in Muslim society in which free intermingling of the sexes is not permitted and in which extra-marital sex is strictly prohibited, it is a matter of grave concern. A medical consultation which disregards these delicate facts is likely to be an unhappy experience for the patient and a difficult exercise for the consultant. The specific situations in which Muslims face difficulties or about which they express concern are (a) medical examination in the surgery of a G.P. or consultant; (b) hospitalization; (c) home visits from hospitals; (d) ante-natal examination and childbirth; (e) the death of Muslim relatives and post mortems.

Medical Examinations

In accordance with Islamic teaching, Muslims are accustomed to being examined by a doctor of their own sex and, whenever possible, this should be arranged. In the event of it not being possible, it is necessary for staff and doctors to show understanding and respect for the Muslim's great concern for modesty and deeply entrenched anxiety when being examined by doctors of the opposite sex. In particular, ante-natal check-ups, childbirth and the exploratory examinations required in the diagnosis of gynaecological diseases cause grave anxiety to women when performed by male doctors. Similarly, diseases which require examination of the male genitalia and anus are likely to cause acute embarrassment when performed by a female doctor. With deep respect to the tremendous pressure placed upon doctors and hospital staff generally, we would, however, suggest that such delicate examination and treatment of Muslim patients should always be performed by a doctor of the same sex.

Hospitalization

In addition to the problems relating to modesty and medical examination, hospitalization presents the Muslim patient with even greater anxiety and tension; in addition to the worry of being in a strange, uniformed and antiseptic environment, which will be common for any patient. It is psychologically and spiritually vital for him to have the opportunity of observing his religious duties, such as the five daily prayers, and of receiving facilities for ablution, bathing and Muslim food.

Prayer

Muslims must pray five times a day; although illness is not an excuse to miss prayer, women at the time of post-natal discharge and monthly periods, and those patients who are mentally ill or deranged are exempt. It is not necessary for the patient to make the usual physical movements, which include standing, bending and prostrating, and a Muslim patient may perform the prayer from his bed. If the patient is not physically or medically restricted to his bed, he should be provided with the facility to pray in one of the corners of the lounge or at a clean and quiet place.

Ablution and Bathing

Cleanliness and purification are essential to Islam. Therefore before any prayer a Muslim will need to ablute with running water and he will require water to clean himself after urination and excretion. Further, a full bath is necessary after seminal discharge or menstruation. If a bath or ablution for prayer endangers the patient's health or is impractical in prevailing circumstances, the patient can take recourse to the concession of *tayammum* – a symbolic act of purification.

MUSLIM FOOD

The avoidance of unlawful food is equally important to the Muslim. In addition to the recommendations made in Chapter 3 on food and drink[1], may we also suggest that the patient's relatives, given the precise dietary requirements and limitations of the particular patient, could be relied upon to co-operate with the hospital authorities by bringing specially prepared food (strictly in accordance with the dietician's advice) for their sick relative.

Home Visits from Hospital

Whilst the whole process of hospitalization can be a very lonely experience for anyone, it can be more distressing for a Muslim faced with communication, cultural and religious problems in a non-Muslim environment. This feeling of isolation reaches a climax at the two major festivals, *'Īd al-Fiṭr* and *'Īd al-Aḍḥā*. Like Christmas and Easter, their celebration does not permeate the environment. These two Islamic festivals are a time for family reunion and special religious services. When the health and treatment of the patient is not at risk, Muslim patients may be allowed to visit their homes during these two festivals. Information on the exact dates can be obtained from the patient or any local Mosque (see Appendix V).

Ante-natal Examination and Childbirth

The nature of ante-natal check-ups, childbirth and certain female diseases necessitate Muslim women visiting and staying in hospital for certain periods of time. In all these

[1] cf pp. 36, 37. See also Chapter 4, section 'Food and Drink', pp. 49, 50. Chapter 5, section, 'Muslim Food' p. 58.

cases, they have to undress and expose their private parts to doctors, surgeons and nurses. In the maternity unit, most of the nurses and junior staff are female, but they have to rely in most cases on male doctors. There are female doctors available in the hospitals, but since the problem does not arise with other women, the hospital authorities do not need to allocate the time of female doctors to women patients. Like male doctors, they are also treating patients of both sexes. Special arrangements can however be made by hospital authorities to allow Muslim female patients to be examined and treated by female doctors and female nursing staff. This arrangement will also be appreciated by the immigrant population belonging to other faiths and perhaps by some of the Christian female patients. The X-ray and various types of tests on expectant mothers should also be preferably done by female staff. If this arrangement can be achieved, a great deal of anxiety on the part of Muslim women can be reduced and some of the causes which complicate and aggravate the problems (e.g. unknown fear and shame of confronting male doctors) will definitely be eliminated. The only special treatment Muslims require from the medical profession is co-operation and a respect for their religion and concern for modesty.

In respect of childbirth, Muslims are often confronted with a very serious problem concerning the Islamic practice of saying the *adhān* (usual call to prayer given from Mosques) into the ears of the baby *immediately* after childbirth. The whole "ceremony" does not take more than 3–4 minutes; either the father or any member of the family stands in front of the baby and calls out the *adhān* in the ear of the baby as a mark of blessing. Sometimes, members of the family prefer to bring along a learned member from the Muslim community to give the *adhān* for the child. The hospital authorities are not always aware of this Islamic religious custom and often appear reluctant to allow a person, other than the husband, to visit the baby outside the visiting hours of the hospital. Muslims will be grateful if the parents are permitted to invite one other person to perform this brief ceremony – simple and short, yet very essential for Muslims.

Death and Post Mortem

If death appears imminent for any Muslim patient, the relatives, or in their absence the Muslim community leader, should be informed and given facilities to perform the customary religious rites. There is no elaborate and complicated ritual to be performed at the death bed. The simple practice which Muslims follow is to sit near the bed of the patient and read some verses from the Qur'ān and pray for the peaceful departure of the soul. If the patient is in a state of consciousness, the Muslims would like him to utter the *Shahādah* (declaration of faith)[1] and breathe his last while reciting these words. This is done to invoke the blessings of Allah and in the hope that Allah will accept his life as a Muslim and forgive his sins in the Hereafter.

After death has occurred, the corpse should be handed over to the relatives or the Muslim community of the locality. They will make arrangements for the washing, shrouding and burial according to Islamic regulations. It should be noted here that Islam requires that the body should be buried as early as possible. There is no truth in the oft-repeated statement that the burial must be performed within twenty-four hours of the death. In fact, it depends on specific circumstances and the time required for the preparation of washing, shrouding and digging of the grave. However, the rule is the sooner the better. Muslims do not usually bury the corpse in a coffin, but if special circumstances or the law requires this, Muslims will not object to adhering to the law.

Unnecessary post mortem of the body is not allowed in Islam. In fact, to do post mortems without the existence of compelling medical or legal circumstances amounts to desecration of the body. It is for this reason that Muslims like to take custody of the remains as early as possible. If relatives or members of the Muslim community are not readily available to take charge of the body, it may be kept in the hospital mortuary for a short period of time. In handling the body, however, care should be taken not to offend Muslim ethics. The female body should be handled by the female staff and the male corpse by the male staff.

[1] On *Shahādah* see Chapter 2. p. 24.

7

Muslims in Penal Institutions

Muslims and the Law

The Muslim is, first and foremost, a servant of Allah and the law to which he is accountable is the law of Islam. This does not mean that a Muslim in Britain is above the law of the state in which he has chosen to live. On the contrary, the Muslim is explicitly urged to comply with statutory and common law so far as it does not force him to break Islamic law and prevent him from performing his Islamic duties.

In relation to legal and social sanctions regarding commonly accepted principles like immorality, indecency, murder, manslaughter, larceny, fraud, etc., British law and Islamic law are not fundamentally at variance in providing sanctions against violation of general principles of social order and morality, except that the concepts, definitions and sanctions may differ. These general principles pertain to such crimes as murder, assault, theft, larceny, fraud. A Muslim should not therefore, if he is a true Muslim, indulge in any of these crimes. However, as previously stated, many Muslims do not follow their religion strictly; without the strength to be obtained from regular prayer and submission to the Will of Allah in every aspect of their life, they become susceptible to their own innate weaknesses and vulnerable to the external influences which act upon them. Consequently, some Muslims find themselves in British courts and penal institutions.

The incidence of non-indictable and indictable crime among Muslims in Britain follows, on a much lower scale, the general pattern for the indigenous population in that crime and delinquency appears to be a predominantly male phenomena, with a higher incidence among teenagers and young adults and mainly confined to petty theft, traffic offences and common assault.

In respect of this fractional minority within the Muslim community, there is no need to defend their misdemeanours and crimes or to conceal the fact of their existence. It is incumbent upon individual Muslims to follow the Divine Path of Islam and peacefully abide by the laws of the country in which they choose to live. Our primary concern in this context is for the spiritual welfare and social rehabilitation of Muslims in custodial care in penal institutions and community homes etc. What we seek is the co-operation of responsible authority to allow Muslims to practise their religion in prisons, remand centres, borstal institutions, community homes and detention centres.

Prayers and Ablutions

Religious observance for Muslims can be incorporated into an effective strategy of social rehabilitation without which their punishment may be perceived as totally retributive. It is on the basis of this belief that the following observations and recommendations are submitted.

However much a Muslim may deviate from his religion, he will never reject, deny or condemn Islam for his own human weaknesses. He will remain a believer and always amenable to assess his own behaviour in an Islamic context.

Prayer is obligatory for all Muslims in all circumstances five times a day at specified times from dawn to late evening.[1]

A Muslim does not require anything more than a prayer mat and a copy of the Qur'ān to meet his obligation to worship and can pray in any clean and quiet place, alone or together with other Muslims (*jamā'ah*). Preceding the prayer, the Muslim must ablute (*wuḍū'*) or, following a nocturnal emission, have a bath or shower; thus access to water is necessary.

(a) Facilities for washing the feet, mouth and nose prepara-

[1] See Chapter 2, pp. 24, 25.

tory to prayer should be provided in a manner which does not create any conflict situation with other non-Muslim inmates.

(b) Muslims are required to avoid nakedness and their modesty in communal showers is likely to invite ridicule and cause tension and embarrassment. They should not, however, be discouraged from wearing trunks in the showers.

When at all possible, Muslims must be encouraged to meet together as a group for prayer, Qur'ān recitations, study groups, meal times and recreation.

Accommodation

As Muslims, and not as an ethnic group, it is recommended that, where at all practicable, Muslims should be accommodated as a separate group as this would facilitate arrangements for collective worship, meals and bathing and ablution.

Food

Bacon or any other food produced from the pig as well as beef, chicken and lamb not slaughtered according to Islamic law should not be consumed by Muslims.[1] Confronted with no other option, a Muslim may restrict himself to a diet of egg, fish, cheese and vegetarian dishes, but this is not desirable for prolonged periods and the prison authorities should take some steps to alleviate his hardship. The special dietary requirements of a Muslim do not impose upon institutional catering staff any greater inconvenience in preparation than the special diets they may be required to prepare for certain inmates, such as diabetics, on medical advice and prescription.

Fasting

Ramaḍān is the month of obligatory fasting from dawn to sunset. Therefore it will be appreciated if arrangements are

[1] For further details on Muslim dietary regulations, see Chapters 3, pp. 36, 37.

made to provide food to Muslim prisoners for their early morning and evening meals (*Suḥūr* and *Ifṭār*). Some prison authorities, such as Gartree prison in Leicestershire, are already helping the Muslim prisoners in procuring Muslim food with the help of the local Muslim organizations. It is hoped that this example will be followed by other prison authorities where there are Muslim prisoners. For specific information about the dietary regulations and Ramaḍān fast, the community leaders and Muslim organizations can be contacted. Some details on Ramaḍān and Muslim food have already been provided in the preceding sections of this guide.[1]

Prison Visits

In the Muslim community, every Muslim is obliged to visit the poor, sick, distressed and prisoners. In a penal institution in Britain, the visitor is important to the Muslim in that he provides a link with the Muslim community from which the prisoner is isolated, and acts as an agent of spiritual, intellectual and social guidance and very often is a highly effective instrument in the Muslim's social rehabilitation; keeping in touch with the family and attending to financial matters and employment possibilities etc. All Muslims are brothers to each other and it is from the existence of this active brotherhood that Muslims can be effectively helped in any circumstances with which, by accident or folly, they are confronted.

Since there is no priesthood in Islam, Muslim prisoners have sometimes been deprived of a visit by Muslims on the grounds that only Muslim priests can come to visit them. Whenever Muslims make contact with prison authorities, the authorities refuse them entry because they do not belong to any "church" or they are not "priests". This is an instance of the ignorance and misinformation about the faith and practices of Muslims prevalent among many. Any Muslim who is well acquainted with religion can lead the prayer in the mosque and can do all the functions that a Christian priest performs. If any lay Muslim is not acceptable to prison

[1] See Chapter 3, Section "Food", pp. 36, 37 and Chapter 5 "Muslims in Employment". Section "Ramaḍān", pp. 56, 57.

authorities for prison visits, the best course will then be to contact the local mosque authorities or any Islamic organization nearby. They can appoint somebody from among themselves who can pay regular visits to Muslim prisoners. It is not necessary that the same person visits all the time; others should also be allowed who possess an authorization letter from a Muslim organization, and who fulfil the requirements of the prison regulations. Therefore, anybody whom the Muslim community recommends should be given access and be provided with all the facilities which a priest in the Christian faith is entitled to. This arrangement can be provided through mutual consultation and co-operation.

Supply of Literature

Books are a good companion of man especially when he is in prison. Muslims, therefore, should also be provided with Islamic literature and books of their choice. The Muslim community will be happy to supply such literature in English and other languages if they are asked to do so.

8

Summary of Recommendations

The following is a brief resumé of the major recommendations emanating from this Guide:

1. Muslims everywhere, especially those in schools and employment, should be helped and encouraged in practising their religion.

2. Prayer is an obligatory duty for every Muslim. Muslims, therefore, should be given a few minutes off to perform their prayers on the premises. On Fridays, however, they should be given some extra time as their lunch recess. Unlike the other prayers, the Friday prayer cannot be offered individually at the place of work.

3. Muslims have a different concept of hygiene and they usually need water to wash their private parts after attending the toilet and for making ablutions before prayers. Provision of water jugs or bottles in toilets and bathrooms will be very helpful.

4. Arrangements for a small prayer room will be helpful in large establishments where sizeable numbers of Muslim workers are in employment, as well as in schools, airports and service stations. Similarly, praying facilities for Muslim shoppers, especially in new shopping complexes, will be a great help, because they find it difficult to go shopping in the afternoon for fear of missing their prayer.

5. Muslim dietary regulations resemble, to a great extent, the Jewish dietary rules. Canteens in schools, colleges, factories and offices should provide *ḥalāl* Muslim food for Muslims, as it is easily available. Even Kosher meat will be acceptable. If *ḥalāl* food is not possible to arrange on certain days, vegetables, fish and eggs may be made available. Muslim food should be cooked in vegetable oil or butter. Use of lard or other animal fats makes the entire food unlawful and unpalatable for Muslims.

6. Muslim students should not be obliged to attend morning assemblies.

7. Muslim students should not be given any sex education which Islam does not approve of, such as practical demonstration of sex organs, sex play or encouragement of sex outside marital bonds.

8. Muslim students should be provided with special facilities for religious instruction.

9. Muslim students should not be asked to wear any form of dress which goes against their religion. In particular, grown-up girl students should be allowed to wear *shalwār* or trousers in place of a skirt.

10. Physical training and swimming are encouraged by Islam, provided the religious requirements are first met. The grown-up girls and boys should not be asked to participate in P.T. and swimming in mixed groups. Grown-up girls are not allowed to uncover any part of their body in front of others, except their faces and hands, whether for P.T., swimming or baths.

11. Muslim patients should be examined and treated by doctors and nurses of their own sex. For female patients in particular, greater care should be taken at the time of ante-natal and post-natal examinations. Expectant mothers feel very embarrassed if they have to undress before and be examined by a male doctor or nurse.

12. On the birth of a child, Islam requires the father or a representative of the family to whisper the call to prayer (*adhān*) in the ear of the new-born child. Facilities for *adhān* should, therefore, be provided immediately after the birth of the baby.

13. If the death of a Muslim patient appears to be imminent, it is customary for the family or their representative to recite verses from the Qur'ān and help the dying patient to recite the *Shahādah* (declaration of faith). The hospital authorities should, therefore, allow the members of the family to be present on the occasion and perform these last rites.

14. When death has occurred, the dead body should be immediately handed over to the family and/or representatives for washing, shrouding and burial. Post mortem, except in exceptional cases, is not allowed in Islam.

15. Since there is no priesthood in Islam, any representative from the mosque or Islamic organizations can visit a prison and perform the functions of a "priest", and should be allowed to do so. Arrangements in this regard can be made by consultation with the Muslim community of the area. The community can also help the authorities in providing Muslim food, give information on the month of fasting (Ramaḍān) and supply Islamic literature to the inmates.

16. The month of Ramaḍān is the month of fasting for every Muslim. Therefore Muslim employees, Muslim students and also prisoners will be fasting as well as carrying out their work responsibilities. Since these employees will not be requiring the lunch and tea breaks, it will be appreciated if employers would consider shortening and adjusting the working hours of their Muslim employees so as to enable them to fulfil this religious obligation without any difficulty.

17. In many situations, Muslims may require special facilities for pre-dawn food (*Suḥūr*) and late night prayers (*tarāwīḥ*).

18. The Festival of *'Īd al-Fiṭr* (which marks the end of the Ramaḍān fast) and *'Īd al-Aḍḥā*, at the time of pilgrimage, are occasions of celebrations for all Muslims. Muslim employees, as well as students, will, therefore, require a day off on these two annual festivals to celebrate the occasion with family, relatives and friends. Muslim patients, if their health permits, should also be given permission to go home and join in the celebration of the festivals. The dates of the two festivals should be marked on calendars as Muslim holidays.

Appendices

I. Some Misconceptions about Islam in the West
Islam is Arabia! – Polygamy – Muslim Women.

II. Glossary of Terms.

III. Islamic Calendar.

IV. Recommended Introductory Reading on Islam.

V. Recommended Courses on Muslim Culture.

VI. List of some Mosques in the United Kingdom and Eire.

VII. List of some important Islamic Organisations in Britain:
(a) International and General
(b) Muslim Institutes
(c) Muslim Women's Associations
(d) Muslim Youth Organisations
(e) Muslim Schools
(f) Muslim Relief Organisations

VIII. Islamic Bookshops and Resource Centres.

APPENDIX I

Some Misconceptions about Islam in the West

Islam is Arabia! – Polygamy – Muslim Women

Myths are weeds that grow in the garden of the mind; unless they are removed truth will never grow. On the subject of Muslim women and Islamic marriage, these myths have grown into a virtual jungle of distortion and misconception. The Muslim world has often been projected by the West as a Disneyland of Arabian Nights and Turkish Delight, in which dark-eyed Sheikhs on Arab stallions charged across the desert carrying off reluctant maidens to exotic harems. Even in these petro-dollar days, there are some highly intelligent Europeans who seriously believe that Muslim women are denied their human rights and are regarded by Muslim men as unintelligent and inferior. Even in Britain there is a startling number of people who really believe that most Muslim men have four wives hidden away in domestic subservience, restricted to a life of toil and unceasing satisfaction of their master's carnal lusts.

Making such contemporary generalizations from historical exceptions may help to provide a television fantasy world into which we can escape from facing reality and confirm our prejudices, but it is seriously detrimental to the promotion of tolerance, understanding and rapport in the plural society of Britain. The propagation of myths serves only to divide us.

The three most outstanding misconceptions, derived from the indiscriminate mass media projection of myth and fantasy, concerning Islam in general and Muslim women in particular revolve around the following inexactitudes and distortions:

(a) Arabia is Islam! – Islam is Arabia!

(b) Polygamy is the common form of Islamic marriage! ("all Muslims have four wives").
(c) Muslim women have no rights! ("Women are the servants of men").

Islam is Arabia!

It is from this popular misconception that most other myths about Muslims are derived.

Islam, a comprehensive spiritual guidance and complete social system, is the Divine path revealed by God for all mankind. The believers of this unique faith are spread throughout the whole of the civilised world and represent every ethnic group and language of the five continents.

Islam, in its final stage, was revealed by God through the Angel Gabriel to Muḥammad (blessings of Allah and peace be upon him) in Arabia and in the Arabic language, over a period of twenty-three years in the seventh century after the Prophet Jesus (blessings of Allah and peace be upon him). From this time, Islam continued to spread with amazing speed, incredible success and with a far reaching influence on all aspects of life, leaving an indelible imprint on the development of science, art and social development in both Muslim and non-Muslim societies. The focal point of Islam to which every Muslim turns to pray is the *Ka'bah* in Makka (Arabia) which was built by the Prophet Abraham (blessings of Allah and peace be upon him) about 4,000 years ago, at the command of God, as an inviolable place of worship to which millions of Muslims make an annual pilgrimage (*Ḥajj*).[1]

Of the nearly one billion Muslims dispersed throughout the world, the combined population of all the Arab-speaking countries is only about 130 million (roughly 15%); Saudi Arabia, Kuwait, Qatar, Bahrain, Oman and the United Emirates, about which there are so many current legends, account for less than 13 million; the whole of North Africa (47 million) and Egypt (33 million), with which Europeans appear to be best acquainted, total approximately 80 million. It is significant that the combined Muslim population of Indonesia (125 million +) and Malaysia (6 million +) is greater,

[1] On *Ḥajj*, see Chapter 2, pp.27–29.

at 131 million, than that of the whole Arab-speaking world. Pakistan, Bangladesh and India account for a further 131 million. In Turkey (38 million) and Iran (32 million) there are 70 million Muslims. The total Muslim population of China incidentally, exceeds the total population of Saudi Arabia. The combined population of Muslims in the communist countries of Europe and the Soviet Union is 81 million and in the non-Arabic speaking countries of Central and South Africa, there are more than 87 million.[1]

From this brief outline of the global spread of Islam, the cultural, ethnic and linguistic diversity of Islam becomes clearly apparent.

Although the Muslim community is inalienably coherent by a commonly shared and actively expressed structure of norms and values, we find within it many variations in customs, traditions and folklore relating to dress, diet, temperament, attitudes, art, occupations, etc., obviously influenced by varied environments. Nevertheless, in respect of modesty, free intermingling of the sexes, family, marriage and morality, this polyglot of nations more or less follow the teachings of the Qur'ān and the example of the Prophet Muḥammad (blessings of Allah and peace be upon him) and do their best to conform to Islamic injunctions and prohibitions without contravention, and within this framework of cultural diversity.

To project contemporary Christianity to the Muslim world in terms of the diabolical activities of some of the Borgia family of Italy, the marital record of Henry VIII, and the European involvement in the African slave trade to America in the eighteenth century would be ludicrous and totally unjust. To accept the equally absurd projection of Islam in Western mass media and literature is similarly irrational and contrary to the successful establishment of economic, social and cultural exchange which prevailing circumstances in the world necessitate.

[1] For full details of the population of the Muslim world, see M.M. Ahsan, *Islam: Faith and Practice*, Islamic Foundation, 1976, Section: Appendix. See also *World Muslim Gazetteer*, Umma Publishing House, Karachi, 1975.

Polygamy

Polygamy, in Islam, is not an imposed and universal form of marriage. It is a Divine concession to the distressing reality of social circumstances such as war, and the surplus of women it creates, childlessness and the chronic sickness of the first wife which can make it necessary and practicable as a prevention and solution of social problems which these unfortunate circumstances would otherwise create. Individuals may face circumstances such as have made extra-marital sex a common occurrence in many societies. Polygamy is socially more secure for women, infinitely fairer to children, legally binding and morally preferable to bigamy, prostitution, mistresses and other similarly permissive patterns of sexual behaviour which appear to threaten the stability and dignity of family life. It certainly reduces the pressures leading to divorce and separation and assures the children a stable family life. However, in the whole of contemporary Islamic society, monogamy is the norm; polygamy is the exception.

In Arabia, Africa, Indonesia, Pakistan, etc., polygamy is very rarely practised by Muslims and most certainly there is little evidence, even as the exception to the rule, that it is prevalent among the settled Muslim community in Britain. Polygamy functions in Islam when the circumstances it was meant to contain prevail; when these circumstances, such as prolonged war etc. do not exist, polygamy ceases to flourish and monogamy is, as now, the norm. The majority of Muslim men are quite content with one wife and the almost negligible number who do practise polygamy do so for the legitimate reasons outlined above, and not from insatiable sexual appetites and for status symbols as legend and myth would have us believe.

Muslim Women

"Muslim women have no freedom, they are slaves to their husbands" declared an English mother as she quickly packed processed food into her shopping bag during a lunchtime break from the factory. "Freedom from what?" asked the young Muslim student in her break from college, "Freedom to share her earnings and wealth with her husband; freedom to share responsibility for keeping the children, freedom to leave the children to roam the streets; freedom to go home and cook and wash and clean after a day at the factory, and still be friendly and a loving wife?"[1]

Equality of the Sexes – Within the Family

The position of men and women in the internal organization of the Muslim family, within the Islamic community in Britain as elsewhere, is clearly defined in the Qur'ān and there is little possibility of role conflict between husband and wife and other adult males and females in this extended family structure. Role obligations and rights naturally conform to the obvious physical differences between men and women and take into account innate abilities and aptitudes. For equality will be a hoax if women have to be on a par with men in every sphere of life and still bear and rear children. In industrial management, it would be called "rational deployment of manpower resources". In the Muslim family it is simply the right person for the right job.

The husband's major responsibility is that of earning all the economic and material needs of the family, thus, in effect, fulfilling his wife's clearly defined right to this provision, without being in any way compelled to contribute financially herself, however independently wealthy she may be. The husband is the head of the family and this, in Islamic terms, quite rightly imposes upon him more obligations than rights. He is more suitable for this obligation, but not the superior member of the team, and his functions are matched to this strength, aptitude, natural inclination and disposition. Many of his responsibilities lie outside the family and, in addition to employment in the community, he has to look after the relations of the family with the rest of society, education, employment, health, social services, housing etc. The father is mainly responsible for the internal discipline of the family, but mostly the power remains delegated to the mother.

The wife's major responsibility is primarily, but not exclusively, concerned with the internal organization of the family;

[1] From an actual conversation reported by a student, in a classroom discussion, to one of the authors.

training and educating the children in an atmosphere of affection and commitment to the spiritual and social values of Islam. The father may supply the materials and general plan of action, but it is the mother who fashions and develops the minds and personalities of the children, creates a home and provides an Islamic refuge of belongingness, security and loyalty for the father and offspring. The mother is indisputably the central pivot around which the whole gamut of family relations revolve and hers is unquestionably a vital and important role which is beyond the natural capabilities and inclinations of men. Children, too, have defined roles and clear responsibilities, and in addition to learning their adult roles without confusion they act (particularly in the Muslim community of Britain) as interpreters and links between two cultures – it is indeed their striving to overcome the difficulties they share that binds them together.

Muslim women in the Islamic community in Britain appear to enjoy their role which, while it is different from that of their husbands, is equally essential. They do not underestimate the importance of their contribution to family stability; they are proud of their status and secure in the knowledge of their many rights. Muslim women meet with each other regularly, informally and formally, and in this way they too make a contribution to linking the family with its focal point – the community, coherent in the common religion which they share and in which they have equality in the eyes of God and men.

Specific Rights of Muslim Women

Contrary to popular opinion in the West, women in Islam have an extensive range of specific rights encompassing: (a) the spiritual; (b) intellectual; (c) social; (d) economic; and (e) political aspects of life. These rights are bestowed on women by God, safeguarded by the infallibility and unique wisdom of the Qur'ān and perpetuated by the sublime example of the Prophet (blessings of Allah and peace be upon him). These rights were granted to women fourteen hundred years ago; they were not grudging concessions to the demands of womens' liberation movements nor a reaction to the heroic, but nevertheless undignified, protestations made by Emily Pankhurst and her dedicated supporters. The most basic right of a woman in Islam is to be accepted as having rights for which she never needs to fight.

Spiritual

Islam does not subscribe to the idea of original sin: and woman, according to the Qur'ān, is not held responsible for Adam's first mistake; both were jointly wrong in their disobedience to God, both repented and both were forgiven. In terms of religious obligations – daily prayers (*Ṣalāh*), fasting (*Ṣawm*), poor dues (*Zakāh*) and pilgrimage (*Ḥajj*) – women have the same duties and are promised the same rewards for carrying them out. However, with compassionate regard to certain physiological situations peculiar to females, women are exempted from prayer and fasting during menstrual periods and forty days after childbirth.

Intellectual

Not only have women a right to full intellectual development but, along with men, they have an obligation to seek knowledge, as the Prophet (blessings of Allah and peace be upon him) said: "It is a duty for every Muslim, male and female, to seek knowledge".

Islam credits women, as also men, with the capacity for learning, understanding, teaching and intellectual development. The knowledge it creates is necessary in the vital process of becoming more conscious of God and for performing the roles that have been assigned, maternal or paternal, domestic or economic. There is nothing at all in Islamic teaching that could be interpreted to mean that Muslim girls or women have less right than Muslim boys or men to an education related to their intelligence, ability, natural inclinations and aptitude; from play school to university, from "O" levels to a doctorate degree.

Within the Muslim community in Britain a high percentage of Muslim girls continue their studies beyond "O" levels and are certainly encouraged to study at "A" level and prepare for University, College and professional/vocational training courses. There is no significant evidence to indicate that Muslim parents in Britain attach more importance to the education of their sons rather than their daughters and to both they appear to give equal freedom of choice in careers, with due regard to the equally important but essentially different primary roles they will play in adult life.

Social

Islamic teaching specifically protects women in all stages of development. However, the most common misconceptions relating to women in the social area are marriage and divorce.

Marriage

Contrary to popular myth, but strictly according to Muslim law, Muslim women cannot be forced to marry without their personal consent and without being consulted at an early stage in the negotiations. The fantasy image of a beautiful young maiden being forced to marry some cruel but rich old man, chosen by her parents, is the "plot" for a fairy story. It is, however, quite true, and according to Islamic teaching, that parents should look for a suitable partner for their children and thus seek to influence them towards a wise decision. In any event, the final decision remains with the boy and girl, because Islamically no marriage can be contracted without the consent of the bride and groom; moreover Islam emphasizes that the marriage partners should see one another before making a final decision. After discussion and negotiation between both sets of parents and agreement about the prospective bride's dowry,[1] meetings and discussions concerning the proposed marriage may take place between the young man and woman. It is important to realize that when a boy or girl gets married they are marrying into an entire extended family – common agreement of both parents and the young couple eliminates the tensions and conflicts commonly associated with "in-laws" in Western society, and contributes to the social cohesion of the Islamic community.

[1] Dowry (*mahr*) in Islam is not, as in certain other cultures, a bride price or symbolic gesture. It is a gift given by the husband to his wife for her exclusive use at the beginning of their married life. It can take the form of money, property or jewellery, etc., and is given strictly according to the husband's means.

The privacy of young married couples is assured, their isolation and independence is never enforced or even encouraged. Marriage in Islam extends a family; it does not fragment it.

Divorce

Islamic teaching strongly disapproves of divorce, but recognizes the existence of marital situations that are irreconcilable and in such cases stipulates provisions for divorce which protect the wife and do least harm to the family as a whole. The initiative for divorce lies in the hands of the husband, but the wife can obtain divorce from a court, even on the plea of dislike of the husband. Also a woman can obtain the right to divorce her husband, without going through legal process, if the marriage contract which binds them has made specific allowance for this contingency.

In all cases the emphasis is on reconciliation which involves the representatives of the two extended families. It is significant that this framework of reconciliation and procedure for divorce has endured in Islamic society for fourteen centuries. Divorce in Islam is a family affair; free from complicated legal procedures and unwarranted publicity, it is not likely to lead to local scandal or national upheaval as is so often the distressing case in Western society.

Economic

Ownership

One of the most fundamental rights of Muslim women is the right to independent ownership. In Islamic law, a woman's right to her own money, land, property and other negotiable assets is indisputably acknowledged and is not subject to change by marriage. This right is equally applied to the property and wealth she has before marriage and any other possessions she requires subsequently.

Transactions

Legally Muslim women are absolutely free to buy, sell, exchange, mortgage or lease the whole or part of their properties, independent of consultation with their husbands and certainly without consent from them.

Income

The whole of a woman's private income, from profits, rents, capital appreciation and earnings etc., belong entirely to her and unless it is her own personal wish, cannot be "absorbed" into the housekeeping or used for general expenses related to the husband's sole responsibility to provide a home, education and welfare for his wife and children. Obviously, in an Islamic marriage, based on love, a rich wife would be inclined to use her wealth, if the husband agreed, to generally raise the quality of life for the whole family. The important thing is that she has the right to decide about this and the husband has *no* right in law to his wife's property, nor in any but the most exceptional cases can he take back gifts, however substantial, that he has made to her; they are absorbed into her own private wealth.

Inheritance

A woman's right to inherit, like her right to property is similarly indisputed, safeguarded and determined in quite minute detail in Islamic law (*Sharī'ah*). A woman's share is, by common practice, about one half of the man's share and, far from implying that a woman is worth only half a man (a popular, yet gross misinterpretation circulated in the West), this division of the parental estate quite justly allocates inherited economic resources in direct relation to economic responsibilities. A woman's wealth, as already stated, is unquestionably her own to spend or accumulate as she wishes. The man in Islamic society is totally responsible for the maintenance of his wife and children and may also have economic responsibilities relating to needy relatives, particularly the females – widows, unmarried sisters, etc.

Employment

There is no decree in Islam which forbids a woman from accepting employment in the community, particularly as doctors, nurses, teachers and other occupations which are compatible with her distinct nature, aptitude and abilities and in no way at variance with the respect and dignity accorded to women in Islam. However, the whole question of employment for Muslim women can only be coherently discussed in relation to the acceptance of women's primary social role in the community as a wife and mother, regarded in Islam as vital and sacred.

Islam recognizes that there are situations in which employment for a woman may be necessary and family circumstances in which the employment of a mother is practicable and not likely to jeopardise family stability. In these cases, Islam encourages women to make their many talents available for the good of the community.

Political

Recorded in history and supported by Islamic teaching, Muslim women have equality with men in political rights. A woman has the right to vote and to be nominated for various political offices and to participate in public affairs at local and national level. What is very important to realize is that Muslim women, who have always had these rights, certainly take advantage of them, and did not have to fight for them. In Islam, many famous women have figured prominently in the affairs of state.

In Britain, within the Muslim community itself and British society as a whole, Muslim women are increasingly taking part in public life and in addition to the Muslim Women's Association in London and many other such societies representing women's interests and opinions etc., they attend, alongside men, public lectures, conferences, seminars, schools and act as magistrates and sit on juries etc. The extent to which Muslim women vote in British elections is determined (as it is for men) by their ability to comprehend the propaganda presented to them.

Conclusions

The rights of Muslim women are entrenched in Islamic history, enshrined in the Qur'ān and made real in life by the obligations imposed on Muslim men. As Gamal Badawi[1] concludes:

(a) The history of Muslims is rich with women of great achievements in all walks of life from as early as the seventh century.
(b) It is impossible for anyone to justify any mistreatment of women by any decree of rule embodied in the Islamic law, nor could anyone dare to cancel, reduce or distort the clear-cut legal rights of women given in Islamic law.
(c) Throughout history, the reputation, chastity and maternal role of Muslim women were objects of admiration by impartial observers.

[1] G. Badawi, "Woman in Islam" in *Islam: Its Meaning and Message*, ed. by K. Ahmad, London, 1975. p. 144.

APPENDIX II

Glossary of Arabic Terms and Some Islamic Greetings and Invocations

Greetings

As-salāmu 'Alaykum	Peace be on you.
Wa 'Alaikum As-Salām	Peace be on you also.
'Īd Mubārak	Congratulations for *'Īd*; Happy *'Īd*.
Khudā Ḥāfiẓ	Goodbye.

Invocations

Allāhu Akbar	Allah is the Greatest.
Alhamdulillāh	Praise be to Allah.
Bismillāh-ir-Rahmān-ir-Raḥīm	In the name of Allah, the Beneficient, the Merciful.
Inshā' Allāh	If Allah should so wish OR God willing.
Jazākallāh Khairan	May Allah reward you for your kindness.
Māshā' Allāh	As may please Allah.
Shukran/Shukriya	Thanks.

Glossary

Adhān	Call to (five daily) prayers.
Ākhirah	The Hereafter.
Arkān	Pillars (of Islam).
'Aṣr	Mid-afternoon prayer, being the third of the five daily pıayers.
'Awrah	The private parts of the body which a Muslim should not expose.
Dunyā	World; worldly life.

Fajr	Early morning prayer – after dawn. This is the first of the five daily prayers.
Farḍ	Obligatory prayer.
Fiqh	Jurisprudence.
Ghusl	Complete bath after sexual intercourse or nocturnal emission.
Hadīth	Reported traditions of the Prophet.
Hajj	Pilgrimage to Makka (Hājī: one who has been on the pilgrimage).
Halāl	Permitted, e.g. *ḥalāl* food.
Harām	Prohibited, e.g. *ḥarām* meat.
Hifẓ	To memorise the Qur'ān.
'Ibādah	Worship in a ritual sense, but all good actions are an act of worship.
'Īd al-Adhā	Festival of sacrifice celebrated by Muslims who do not go for *ḥajj* or pilgrimage to Makka.
'Īd al-Fitr	Festival of breaking the fast celebrated at the end of Ramaḍān on the first day of the Islamic month, Shawwal.
Ifṭār	Breaking the fast after sunset.
Imām	The person who leads the prayer: a religious leader.
Imān	Faith, conviction.
'Ishā'	Evening prayer – usually recommended before midnight, being the last of the five daily prayers.
Islām	The word in Arabic derives from the root SLM and denotes submission and peace.
Jamā'ah	Congregational prayer.
Jihād	To struggle and strive for Islam – it is both an internal and external struggle.
Jum'ah	Friday.
Salātul Jum'ah	Friday congregational prayer.
Ka'bah	The House of Allah – focal point in Makka towards which all Muslims turn for prayer.
Khalīfah	God's representative on earth (an honour given to man by God); the Caliph or head of the Muslim government.
Maghrib	Prayer just after sunset, being the fourth of the five daily prayers.

Mahr	Dowry paid by the husband to the wife. It is a compulsory part of the marriage contract and an exclusive property of the wife.
Makrūh	Not actually forbidden by Islamic practice, but strongly discouraged.
Mandūb	Recommended, but not enjoined.
Mubāḥ	Permitted through silence.
Qārī	A reciter of the Qur'ān (who usually reads the Qur'ān in a melodious voice with proper rules of *al-Tajwid* (the science of recitation of the Qur'ān).
Qiblah	The direction towards which Muslims face in their prayers.
Qur'ān	Literally, reading. The last Divine Revelation of Allah.
Ramaḍān	The Muslims' sacred month of fasting, the ninth month of the Muslim lunar calendar.
Rasūl	Messenger – Rasūlallāh – Messenger of Allah.
Risālah	The Prophethood, beginning with Adam and finalised by Muḥammad.
Sadaqah al-Fiṭr	The money paid to the needy before *'Īd al-Fiṭr* by those who can afford, to enable the poor to participate in *'Īd* festivities.
Salāh	Ritual prayer.
Sawm	Fasting – particularly in Ramaḍān, but recommended at other times as well.
Shahādah	Testimony – declaration of belief in the Oneness of Allah (*Tawḥīd*).
Shalwār	Trousers usually used by Pakistani/Indian Muslim women.
Sharī ah	Islamic law contained within the Qur'ān and the *Sunnah*.
Suhūr	Early morning meal taken before dawn (by a person who intends to fast).
Sunnah	The reported traditions and sayings of the Prophet.
Tarāwīḥ	Special night prayers during the month of Ramaḍān.
Tawhīd	Unity – the basic concept of Islamic teaching – Oneness of Allah.

Tayammum	The symbolic purification before prayer when running water is not available.
'Umrah	Lesser Pilgrimage. Can be performed any time other than the days of *Ḥajj*.
Wājib	Expressly enjoined.
Wuḍū'	Ritual washing (purification) before prayers.
Zakāh	Welfare due, given annually to the poor and distressed.
Ẓuhr	Midday prayer, being the second of the five daily prayers.

APPENDIX III

Islamic Calendar

1399 A.H. – After *Hijrah*, the migration of the Prophet Muḥammad.

1979 A.C. – After the Prophet Jesus.

The Muslim era began with the Great Event of the *Hijrah* or the migration of the Prophet Muḥammad and his Companions from Makka to Madina.

The Muslim calendar is lunar, and its months are determined by the various positions of the moon. In every year, there are twelve months, and each month is either thirty or twenty-nine days depending on the position of the moon, thus making the Muslim year approximately eleven days shorter than the Christian Gregorian one. Unlike the Christian and Jewish calendar, the *Hijrī* months do not correspond with the four seasons, but begin slightly earlier each year. For instance, if in a given lunar year the fasting of Ramaḍān and *'Īd* Festival occur during the heat of the summer, they will occur within the cool season 16¼ years later, which means that in each 32½ years, the *Hijrī* year passes through all the solar seasons. In this way, one hundred Muslim *Hijrī* years will approximately be equal to only ninety-seven years of the Christian Gregorian calendar. These Islamic months are: Muḥarram, Safar, Rabī' Al-Awwal, Rabī' Al-Thānī, Jumādah Al-Ūlā, Jumādah Al-Thāniyah, Rajab, Sha'bān, Ramaḍān, Shawwāl, Dhul-Qa'dah and Dhul-Ḥijjah.

The following is the list of important events in the Islamic calendar:[1]

(i) The first day of Muḥarram is the New Years Day in the Islamic Calendar.
(ii) The Prophet's birthday which falls on the twelfth day of Rabīʿ Al-Awwal.
(iii) Ramaḍān, the Month of Fasting, in which the Qur'ān was revealed.
(iv) The Night of Power or *Qadr (Lailatul Qadr)* celebrated generally on the twenty-seventh of Ramaḍān.
(v) *ʿĪd al-Fiṭr* (Festival of Breaking the Fast of Ramaḍān) celebrated on the first day of Shawwāl.
(vi) *ʿĪd al-Aḍḥā* (Festival of Sacrifice) which falls on the tenth day of Dhul-Ḥijjah.

[1] Islamic calendar containing information on prayer timings, Ramaḍān, festivals, etc., can be obtained from local Muslim organizations and Islamic bookshops. Dates of important Islamic events may also be obtained from the calendars published by the local Community Relations Council.

APPENDIX IV

Recommended Introductory Reading on Islam

Qur'ān

1. *The Holy Qur'ān* (Arabic text, English translation and commentary) – Abdullah Yusuf Ali. Islamic Foundation, 1978.
2. *The Qur'ān: Basic Teachings* (An anthology of selected passages from the Qur'ān, translated into contemporary English with an Introduction to the Message of the Qur'ān) – T.B. Irving, K. Ahmad, M.M. Ahsan. Islamic Foundation, 1979.
3. *'Ulūm al-Qur'ān: An Introduction to the Sciences of the Qur'ān* – Ahmad von Denffer. Islamic Foundation, 1984.
4. *Way to the Qur'ān* – Khurram Murad. Islamic Foundation, 1985.
5. *Qur'ān for Children.* – Abdur Rauf. Ferozsons Ltd., Lahore.

Ḥadīth

1. *Sahīh al-Bukhārī* – text and English translation by Muhsin Khan. 9 vols.
2. *Sahīh al-Muslim* – English translation by Abdul Hameed Siddiqi. 4 vols. Lahore, 1971–75.
3. *Mishkāt al-Maṣābīh* – English translation by James Robson. 4 vols.
4. *Riyādh-us-Sāleheen* of al-Nawawi – English translation by S.M. Qadri Abbasi. Karachi, 1983. Another translation by the Qadiyani Zafrullah Khan, *Gardens of the Righteous*. Curzon Press, 1975.

5. Al-Nawawi's *Forty Ḥadīth* – English translation by Ezzedin Ibrahim and D.J. Davies. Syria, 1976.
6. *Moral Rectitude* – Rahim Ali Al-Hashimi. Published by the Board of Islamic Publications, Delhi, 1972.
7. *Glimpses of the Ḥadīth* – M. Azizullah. Karachi, 1965.
8. *A Day with the Prophet* – Ahmad von Denffer. Islamic Foundation, 1979.
9. *The 200 Hadith: 200 Sayings and Doings of the Prophet Muhammad (may peace be upon Him)* – Selected and Revised by Abdul Rahim Alfahim. 1988.
10. *Introduction to Ḥadīth: The Traditions of the Prophet Muhammad* – A. Rahman Doi. Lagos, 1981.

Life and Time of the Prophet

1. *The Life of Muhammad* – Abdul Hamid Siddiqi. Lahore, 1969.
2. *Muhammad* – H. Haykal, English translation by Ismail Faruqi. American Trust Publications, 1978.
3. *The Benefactor* – Waheeduddin Faqir. Crescent Publications, Washington, 1973.
4. *Muhammad: Blessings for Mankind* – Afzalur Rahman. London, 1979.
5. *Muhammad: His Life Based on the Earliest Sources* – Martin Lings. London, 1983.
6. *Muhammad Rasūlullah* – M. Hamidullah. Hyderabad, 1974.
7. *Muhammad: The Benefactor* – Naim Siddiqi. Lahore, 1974.
8. *Muhammad: Aspects of His Biography* – Ziauddin Sardar. Islamic Foundation, Leicester, 1978.
9. *The Makkan Crucible* – Zakaria Bashier. Islamic Foundation, Leicester, 1991.
10. *Hijra: Story and Significance* – Zakaria Bashier. Islamic Foundation, Leicester, 1983.
11. *Sunshine at Madina: Studies in the Life of the Prophet Muhammad* – Zakaria Bashier. Islamic Foundation, Leicester, 1990.

General

1. *Islam: Its Meaning and Message* – Khurshid Ahmad. Islamic Foundation, 1976.

2. *Towards Understanding Islam* – S. Abul A'la Mawdudi. Islamic Foundation, 2nd revised edition, 1980.
3. *Islam in Focus* – Hammudah Abdalati. International Islamic Federation of Student Organizations (IIFSO), 1978.
4. *Let us be Muslims* – S. Abul A'la Mawdudi. Islamic Foundation, Leicester, 1985.
5. *Muslims in the West: The Message and Mission* – Syed Abul Hasan Ali Nadwi. Islamic Foundation, Leicester, 1983.
6. *Islam: Beliefs and Teachings* – Ghulam Sarwar. London, 1982.
7. *Introduction to Islam* – M. Hamidullah. London, 1979.
8. *Islam: Faith and Practice* – M. M. Ahsan. Islamic Foundation, 1976.
9. *Islam: Basic Principles and Characteristics* – K. Ahmad, Islamic Foundation, 1977.
10. *Introducing Islam from Within: Alternative Perspectives* – Mona Abul-Fadl. Islamic Foundation, Leicester, 1991.
11. *Islamic Law and Constitution* – Abul A'la Mawdudi. Lahore, 1960.
12. *Family Life in Islam* – Khurshid Ahmad. Islamic Foundation, 1976.
13. *Woman in Islam* – Aisha Lemu and Fatima Heeren. Islamic Foundation, Leicester, 1978.
14. *The Family Structure in Islam* – Hammudah Abal al-Ati. American Trust Publications, Indiana, 1978.
15. *Inner Dimensions of Islamic Worship* – al-Ghazali, English translation by M. Holland. Islamic Foundation, Leicester, 1983.
16. *Sharī'ah: The Way to God* – Khurram Murad. Islamic Foundation, 1981.
17. *Sharī'ah: The Way of Justice* – Khurram Murad. Islamic Foundation, 1985.
18. *Sacrifice: The Making of a Muslim* – Khurram Murad. Islamic Foundation, 1985.
19. *Islam and the Economic Challenge* – M. Umer Chapra. Islamic Foundation, Leicester, 1992.
20. *Studies in Islamic Economics* – ed. Khurshid Ahmad. Islamic Foundation, 1981.
21. *Banking Without Interest* – M. N. Siddiqi. Islamic Foundation, Leicester, 1983.

For Children and Schools

1. *The Children's Book of Islam,* Part One and Part Two – M. M. Ahsan.
2. *Islam for Children* – Ahmad von Denffer. Islamic Foundation, 1982.
3. *Muslim Nursery Rhymes* – M. Y. McDermott. Islamic Foundation, 1982.
4. *Assalamu Alaikum.* Islamic Foundation, 1982.
5. *A Great Friend of Children.* Islamic Foundation, 1982.
6. *Love all Creatures.* Islamic Foundation, 1981.
7. *Love Your Brother, Love Your Neighbour* – Khurram Murad. Islamic Foundation, 1982.
8. *Love Your God* – Khurram Murad. Islamic Foundation, 1982.
9. *The Brave Boy* – M. S. Kayani and Khurram Murad. Islamic Foundation, 1982.
10. *Stories of the Caliphs* – Khurram Murad and M. S. Kayani. Islamic Foundation, 1982.
11. *Marvellous Stories from the Life of Muhammad* – Mardijah A. Tarantino. Islamic Foundation, 1982.
12. *Abu Bakr: The First Caliph* – Muhammad Rashid Feroze. Islamic Foundation, 1982.
13. *A Time to Speak – Anecdotes from Sadi Shirazi* – ed. Ashraf Abu Turab and Ziauddin Sardar. Islamic Foundation, 1980.
14. *Muslim Crossword Puzzles* – Arshad Gamiet. Islamic Foundation, 1981.
15. *Love at Home* – Khurram Murad. Islamic Foundation, 1983.
16. *The Kingdom of Justice: Stories from the life of Umar* – Khurram Murad. Islamic Foundation, 1983.
17. *The Persecutor Comes Home: Story of Umar* – Khurram Murad. Islamic Foundation, 1985.
18. *The Longing Heart: Story of Abu Dhar* – Khurram Murad. Islamic Foundation, 1985.
19. *The Long Search: Story of Salman the Persian* – Khurram Murad. Islamic Foundation, 1984.
20. *The Desert Chief: Story of Thumama Ibn Uthal* – Khurram Murad. Islamic Foundation, 1984.
21. *The Broken Idol and the Jewish Rabbi* – Khurram Murad. Islamic Foundation, 1985.

22. *The Wise Poet: Story of Al-Tufayl bin 'Amr* – Khurram Murad. Islamic Foundation, 1985.
23. *The Courageous Children* – Ayesha Abdullah Scott. Islamic Foundation, 1989.
24. *Muslim Poems for Children* – Mymona Hendricks. Islamic Foundation, 1991.
25. *Tales of Mercy* – Anwar Cara. Islamic Foundation, 1992.
26. *New Friends, New Places* – Susan Omar. Islamic Foundation, 1993.
27. *Islam for Younger People* – Ghulam Sarwar. London.
28. *Children's Book on Salah* – Ghulam Sarwar. London.
29. *The Prophets* – Syed Ali Ashraf. London.
30. *Travellers and Explorers.*

Teaching Aids

	Posters	*Publisher*
1.	Set of four Islamic posters 16″ × 12″	The Islamic Foundation
2.	Prophet Muhammad at Makka 27¼″ × 21¾″	The Islamic Foundation
3.	Prophet Muhammad at Madina 27¼″ × 21¾″	The Islamic Foundation
4.	Three Most Sacred Places of Islam 25″ × 17″	The Muslim Educational Trust
5.	Five Basic Duties of Islam 25″ × 17″	The Muslim Educational Trust
6.	Prophets of Allah Mentioned in the Qur'ān 25″ × 17″	The Muslim Educational Trust
7.	How to Make Wuḍū' and How to Perform Ṣalāh 25″ × 17″	The Muslim Educational Trust

	Maps	
1.	Map of the Muslim World 29½″ × 18″	The Islamic Foundation
2.	Muslim World Map 40″ × 28″	The Islamic Foundation

Audio Visual

1. *Islam: The Way of Peace* – A. Hamid and K. Murad. (34 slides, cassette and notes – running time 10 minutes). Islamic Foundation, 1982.
2. *Muslim Children's Stories: Love All Creatures* – narrated by Yusuf Islam and Maryam Davies (cassette). Islamic Foundation, 1985.
3. *A Guide to the Mosque* (video tape VHS). Available from Islamic Foundation.
4. *Film on Hajj* – Saudi Arabian Ministry of Information.
5. *Prayer breathes life into the souls* (video tape). Muslim Information Services.
6. *Islam: a pictorial essay,* in four parts (video tape VHS and Betamax). Islamic Texts Society.

Audio-Cassettes

Muslim Children's Stories – K. Murad and M.S. Kayani – narrated by Zia Mohyeddin. Age group 8–11 years. Sold separately or as an album of 14 cassettes. Islamic Foundation.

Islamic Games for Children

A New Game of Snakes and Ladders for Muslim Children. Islamic Foundation.

Personal Computer Islamic Quiz Game

The first quality Islamic game on PC for everyone. It will increase your Islamic knowledge on the Qur'ān, Sirah, Ummah, Events and Fiqh. IBM PC or 100% compatible with minimum 512 KB RAM. $3^1/_2$" or $5^1/_4$" Floppy Drive. EGA or VGA display. MS-DOS version 2.0 or higher. Islamic Foundation. 1992.

Transparencies

35mm Slides/Colour Transparencies

Slides for educational and research use. More than 10,000 slides on Islamic heritage and architecture, Islamic art and calligraphy, nature, mosques around the world and Muslim life. Also available to publishing media. For further details please write to Audio-Visual Unit, Islamic Foundation.

APPENDIX V

Recommended Courses on Muslim Culture

The Education and Training Unit of the Islamic Foundation has been running cultural awareness courses since early 1991. These well-structured courses are of both residential and non-residential types and organised on-site as well as in-house. The courses have proved to be very effective for professionals working with Muslims in developing their understanding and awareness of the issues involved.

The courses are based on thoroughly researched information and presented by experienced tutors and trainers. A visit to an on-site Islamic Exhibition and a tour of the local mosque and community centre are added benefits.

The courses are conducted in small groups. The participants are awarded a certificate of attendance. It is ideal for personnel involved in equal-opportunities work, education, community, social services, counselling, health, police force, probation and other areas where they have to deal and work with Muslims.

For further information please contact:

The Training Unit,
The Islamic Foundation,
Ratby Lane, Markfield,
Leicester LE67 9RN, UK.
Tel: 0530 244944/5
Fax: 0530 244946

APPENDIX VI

Some Mosques in Britain

In Britain, the major Islamic institutions are the mosques where prayer, children's Islamic education and community activities are performed. There are about one thousand mosques scattered all over Britain; listed below are some of the important ones in major British cities.

Birmingham

180 Belgrave Road, Birmingham 12	021 440 4037
523 Coventry Road, Birmingham 10	021 772 6408
179 Anderton Road, Birmingham B11 1NQ	021 773 8651
20 Green Lane, Small Heath, Birmingham 9	021 773 0019
23 Arden Road, Birmingham 6	021 551 0887
9 Serpentine Road, Birmingham 6	021 328 0837
423 Stratford Road, Birmingham 11	021 773 8301
401–403 Alum Rock Road, Birmingham B8 3DT	021 326 9930
27 Putney Road, Handsworth, Birmingham B20 3PP	021 551 9012

Blackburn

29 Bicknell Street, Blackburn	0254 54318
71 Saunders Road, Blackburn BB2 6LS	0254 698609

Bradford

30 Howard Street, Bradford 5	
28 Shearbridge Road, Bradford 7	0274 305654

Bristol

1 Green Street, Totterdown, Bristol BS3 4UB

Cambridge

175 Chesterton Road, Cambridge	0223 50134
17 Hills Road, Cambridge	0223 54605

Cardiff
1 Alice Street, Bute Town, Cardiff 0222 25830
17 Peel Street, Cardiff
Severn Road, Canton, Cardiff
1 Tydfil Place, Roath Park, Cardiff 0222 495587

Coventry
Eagle Street, Hillfields, Coventry 0203 222169

Derby
7 Hastings Street, Derby 0332 766237

Dewsbury
7–11 Saville Grove, Dewsbury 0924 461427
South Street, Dewsbury 0924 460760

Dublin
163 South Circular Road, Dublin 8 0001 753242/532785

Dundee
114 Hilltown, Dundee 0382 28374

Edinburgh
12 Roxburgh Street, Edinburgh 031 556 1902

Glasgow
Central Mosque and Islamic Centre, Glasgow 041 429 3132
19 Carrington Street, Glasgow G3 041 331 1119

Huddersfield
32 Upper George Street, Huddersfield

Leeds
48 Spencer Place, Leeds LS7 4BR 0532 680746

Leicester
Asfordby Street, Leicester 0533 621963
2A Sutherland Street, Leicester 0533 854052
3–9 Keythorpe Street, Leicester 0533 511833
55 Upper Tichbourne Street, Leicester 0533 543887
146–152 Berners Street, Leicester 0533 622640

Liverpool
29 Hatherley Street, Liverpool 8 051 709 2560

London

Central Mosque, 146 Park Road, London NW8	071 724 3363
84–92 Whitechapel Road, London E1 1DL	071 247 1357
59 Brick Lane, London E1	071 247 4969
264 Dunsford Road, London SW19	081 946 3350
13–15 Thomas Road, Finsbury Park, London N4	071 226 7070
70 Cazenove Road, Stoke Newington, London N16	081 806 6540
47–51 Balham High Road, London SW17	081 675 0416
16 Ford Square, London E1	071 790 0693
Dacre Road, London E11	081 539 7251
9 Christian Street, London E1	071 481 1294
266–268 High Street North, London E12	081 472 2745
30–32 Ransom Road, London SE7	081 858 4479
295 Barking Road, East Ham, London E6 1LB	081 471 9355

Ilford

54–56 Albert Road, Ilford	081 478 3115

Luton

2 Westbourne Road, Luton, Beds.	0582 34988

Manchester

32 Upper Park Road, Victoria Park, Manchester M14	061 224 4119
3 Woodlands Road, Cheetham Hill, Manchester M8	061 740 3696
443 Cheetham Hill Road, Manchester M8 7PF	061 740 3351
2 Barlow Road, Leveshulme, Manchester M19 3DJ	061 224 5143

Middlesbrough

Waterloo Road, Middlesbrough

Nelson

4–8 Forest Street, Nelson, Lancs.	0282 694471

Newcastle-upon-Tyne

Malvern Street, Newcastle-upon-Tyne NE4 6SU	091 273 8549
1 Rothburn Terrace, Newcastle-upon-Tyne NE6 5XH	091 265 4083

Norwich

Chapelfield East, Norwich	0603 23337

Nottingham

163 Woodborough Road, Nottingham NG3 1AX	0602 582973

Nuneaton

Frank Street, Nuneaton	0203 382372

Oldham	
44 Manchester Road, Werneth, Oldham OL9 7AP	061 678 6772
77 Retford Street, Goldwick, Oldham OL4 1BL	061 628 4472
Oxford	
18 Bath Street, Oxford	
Peterborough	
311 Cromwell Road, Peterborough PE1 2HP	0733 51759
Preston	
Porter Street, Preston	0772 54578
18 Clarendon Street, Preston PR1 3YN	0772 57127
Rochdale	
25 Hare Street, Rochdale OL11 1JL	0706 48094
Rugby	
88 Grosvenor Road, Rugby	0788 3680
Sheffield	
24 Wolseley Road, Sheffield 8	0742 585021
13 Industrial Road, Sheffield S9 5FP	0742 41500
Roundel Street, Sheffield S9 3LE	0742 430102
Slough	
106 St. Paul's Avenue, Slough, Berks. SL2 5BR	0723 20607
Southampton	
189 Northumberland Road, Southampton	0703 35941
Sunderland	
73 Chester Road, Sunderland	
Walsall	
4 Rutter Street, Walsall WS1 4HN	0922 20982
Woking	
149 Oriental Road, Woking	0483 60679
Wolverhampton	
213 Newhampton Road East, Wolverhampton	0902 711304

APPENDIX VII

Islamic Organisations

(a) International and General

1. Islamic Council of Europe,
   16 Grosvenor Crescent,
   LONDON SW1 7EP
   Tel. 071 235 9832

2. U.K. Islamic Mission,
   202 North Gower Street,
   LONDON NW1 2LY
   Tel. 071 387 2157

3. Dawatul Islam,
   52 Fieldgate Street,
   LONDON E1 1ES
   Tel. 071 247 0689

4. Federation of Students' Islamic Societies in U.K. & Eire (FOSIS),
   38 Mapesbury Road,
   LONDON NW2 4JD
   Tel. 081 452 4493

5. Union of Muslim Organizations,
   109 Campden Hill Road,
   LONDON NW8
   Tel. 071 221 6608
   071 229 0538

6. Confederation of Sunni Mosques (Midlands),
   107 Golden Hillock Road,
   BIRMINGHAM 10
   Tel. 021 622 1369
   021 328 0837

7. Markazi Jamiat Ahle Hadith,
   20 Green Lane,
   Small Heath,
   BIRMINGHAM B9 5DB
   Tel. 021 773 0019

8. Islamic Circle Organization,
   2 Digswell Street,
   LONDON N7 8LR
   Tel. 071 607 6655

9. The Muslim World League,
   46 Goodge Street,
   LONDON W1E 4EZ
   Tel. 071 636 7569

10. UK Action Committee on Islamic Affairs,
    146 Park Street,
    LONDON NW8 7RG
    Tel. 081 974 2780
    Fax 081 974 2788

11. South London Islamic Centre,
8 Mitcham Lane,
LONDON SW16 6NN
Tel. 01 677 0588

12. Al-Quran Society,
101 Belmont Road,
LONDON N17 6AT
Tel. 081 889 6662

13. Islamic Forum Europe,
45 Brick Lane,
LONDON E1 6PU
Tel. 071 375 0735

14. International Majlis Khatme Nubuwat,
35 Stockwell Green,
LONDON SW9 9HZ
Tel. 071 737 8199

15. Islamic Society of Britain,
Markfield Conference Centre,
Ratby Lane, Markfield,
LEICESTER LE67 9RN
Tel. 0530 244944

16. Council for Mosques,
6 Claremont,
BRADFORD BD7 1BQ
Tel. 0274 732479

17. Hizbul Ulama UK
(Society of Muslim Scholars),
7 Troy Street,
BLACKBURN BB1 6NY
Tel. 0254 663317

18. Muslim Parliament,
6 Endsleigh Street,
LONDON WC1H 0DS
Tel. 071 388 2581

19. Islamic Party of Britain,
PO Box 844,
Oldbrook,
MILTON KEYNES MK 2TT
Tel. 0908 671756

(b) Muslim Institutes

1. The Islamic Foundation,
Markfield Dawah Centre,
Ratby Lane, Markfield,
LEICESTER LE67 9RN
Tel. 0530 244944

2. The Muslim Institute,
6 Endsleigh Road,
LONDON WC1H 0DS
Tel. 071 388 2581

3. Muslim Educational Trust,
130 Stroud Green Road,
LONDON N4 3RZ
Tel. 071 272 8502

4. Islamic Texts Society,
5 Green Street,
CAMBRIDGE CB1 3JU
Tel. 0223 314387

5. The Islamic Academy,
   23 Metcalfe Road,
   CAMBRIDGE CB4 2DB
   Tel. 0223 350976

6. The Islamic Academy of Manchester,
   19 Chorlton Terrace,
   off Upper Brook Street,
   Brunswick,
   MANCHESTER M13 9TD
   Tel. 061 273 1145

7. Muslim College,
   20 Creffield Road,
   LONDON W5 3RP
   Tel. 081 992 6636

8. International Institute of Islamic Thought,
   40 London House,
   253 Lower Mortlake Road,
   RICHMOND,
   Surrey TW9 2UD
   Tel. 081 948 5166
   Fax 081 940 4014

9. Oxford Centre for Islamic Studies,
   St. Cross College,
   OXFORD OX1 3TO
   Tel. 0856 725077

10. Muslim Education Forum,
    93 Court Road,
    Balsall Heath,
    BIRMINGHAM B12 9LQ
    Tel. 021 440 3500
    Fax 021 440 8144

11. Muslim Children's Home,
    Madina House,
    146 Gloucester Place,
    LONDON NW1 6DT
    Tel. 071 262 5314

12. Muslim Education Co-ordinating Council,
    7 Paul Gardens,
    EAST CROYDON,
    Surrey CR0 5QL
    Tel. 081 681 6087

(c) Muslim Women's Organisations

1. U.K. Islamic Mission,
   Women's Wing,
   83 Gladstone Road,
   Sparkbrook,
   BIRMINGHAM B11
   Tel. 021 771 2780

2. Dawatul Islam London Branch – Ladies Circle,
   52 Fieldgate Street,
   LONDON E1 1ES
   Tel. 071 377 6975

(d) Muslim Youth Organisations

1. Young Muslims Organization (YMO),
   54 Fieldgate Street,
   LONDON E1 1ES
   Tel. 071 247 7918

2. YMO Birmingham,
   523–525 Coventry Road,
   Small Heath,
   BIRMINGHAM B10 0LL
   Tel. 021 772 6408/3014

3. YMO Bradford,
14 Nesfield Street,
BRADFORD BD1 3DA
Tel. 0274 729418

4. National Association
of Muslim Youth,
Markfield Dawah Centre,
Ratby Lane, Markfield,
LEICESTER LE67 9RN
Tel. 0530 244951

5. The Muslim Youth Movement,
8 Caburn Road,
HOVE BN3 6EF
Tel. 0273 722438

6. The Young Muslims U.K.
Markfield Dawah Centre,
Ratby Lane, Markfield,
LEICESTER LE67 9RN
Tel. 0530 244951

7. YMs,
443 Cheetham Hill Road,
MANCHESTER M8 7PF
Tel. 061 740 3351

8. Muslim Youth Foundation,
27 Turner Street,
MANCHESTER M4 1DY
Tel. 061 832 5352

(e) Muslim Schools

1. Al-Furqan School,
Stanfield House,
447 Warwick Road,
Tyseley,
BIRMINGHAM B11 2JR
Tel. 021 764 5373

2. Zakaria Muslim Girls' High School,
111 Warwick Road,
WAKEFIELD
West Yorkshire WF17 6AJ
Tel. 0924 444217

3. Birmingham Al-Hijra School,
Midland House,
Hob Moor Road,
Small Heath,
BIRMINGHAM B10 0LL
Tel. 021 766 5454
Fax 021 766 8556

4. Dewsbury Institute of Islamic Education,
South Street,
Savile Row,
DEWSBURY,
West Yorkshire WF12 9NG
Tel. 0924 455762

5. London Islamic College,
16 Settles Street,
LONDON E1 1JP
Tel. 071 377 1595

6. London Al-Muntada Al-Islami School,
7 Bridges Place,
off Parson Green Lane,
LONDON SW6 4HR
Tel. 071 736 9060
Fax 071 736 4255

7. Malvern Al-Isra Islamic College,
Heathland,
Upper Welland Road,
MALVERN,
Worcestershire WR14 4HN
Tel. 0684 892300

8. Madinatul Uloom Islamiya,
near KIDDERMINSTER,
West Midlands

9. Leicester Islamic Academy,
320 London Road,
LEICESTER
Tel. 0533 705343

10. Jameah Islamiya,
147 Kentiman Road,
LONDON SW8 1JZ
Tel. 071 735 9635
Tel. 081 674 6720

11. Darul Uloom Islamic High School,
521 Coventry Road,
Small Heath,
BIRMINGHAM B10 0LL
Tel. 021 772 6408
021 773 7706

12. Tauheedul Islam Girls' High School,
31 Bicknell Street,
BLACKBURN BB1 7EY
Tel. 0254 54021/677654

13. Muslim Girls' School,
High Street (off Derby Street),
BOLTON BL3 6TA
Tel. 0204 361103

14. Madni Muslim Girls' High School,
1–3 Thornie Bank,
off Scarborough Street,
Savile Town,
DEWSBURY,
West Yorkshire WF12 9AX
Tel. 0924 468516

15. Darul Uloom Al-Arabiya Al-Islamiya,
Holcombe Hall,
HOLCOMBE,
nr. Bury,
GMC,
BL8 4NG
Tel. 070 682 6106

16. Islamia Primary School,
8 Brondesbury Park,
LONDON NW6 7BT
Tel. 081 451 4547

17. Islamia Girls' School,
184 Walm Lane,
LONDON NW2
Tel. 081 208 3531

(f) Muslim Relief Organisations

1. Muslim Aid,
PO Box 3,
LONDON N7 8LR
Tel. 071 609 4425/4426
Fax 071 609 4943

2. Islamic Relief,
19 Rea Street
BIRMINGHAM B5 6LB
Tel. 021 622 6477
Fax 021 622 5003

3. Human Appeal International,
PO Box 61,
MANCHESTER M16 7PP
Tel. 061 237 1101
Fax 061 237 1102

4. Children's Relief Fund,
Markfield Conference Centre,
Ratby Lane, Markfield,
LEICESTER LE67 9RN
Tel. 0530 244944/5
Fax 0530 244946

7. Malvern Al Isra Islamic College

[illegible]

Upper Welland Road,
MALVERN,
Worcestershire WR14 4HN
Tel. 0684 892500

8. Madinatul Uloom Islamia
near KIDDERMINSTER,
West Midlands

9. Leicester Islamic Academy,
320 London Road,
LEICESTER
Tel. 0533 705343

10. Jameah Islameah,
117 [illegible] Road,
LONDON SW9 1JZ
Tel. 071 [illegible]
Tel. 081 [illegible]

11. [illegible] High [illegible]

[illegible] Coventry Road
Small Heath,
BIRMINGHAM B10 0LL
Tel. 021 772 6408
[illegible]

12. Tauheedul Islam Girls' High School,
31 Beckwith Street,
BLACKBURN BB1 1LY
Tel. 0254 54902/661654

13. Muslim Girls' School,
High Street (off Derby Street)
BOLTON BL3 6TA
Tel. 0204 36112

14. Madni Muslim Girls' High School,
[illegible] Church Bank,
off Scarborough Street,
Savile Town,
DEWSBURY
West Yorkshire WF12 9AX
Tel. 0924 468516

15. Darul Uloom Al Arabiya Al-Islamiya,
Holcombe Hall
HOLCOMBE
nr. Bury
GMC
BL8 4NG
Tel. 070 682 6106

16. Islamia Primary School
8 Brondesbury Park,
LONDON NW6 7BT
Tel. 081 451 4547

17. Islamia Girls' School,
[illegible] Walm Lane,
LONDON [illegible]
Tel. 081 [illegible]

(d) Muslim Relief Organisations

1. Muslim Aid
PO Box [illegible]
LONDON [illegible]
Tel. 071 [illegible]
Fax 071 [illegible]

[illegible]
[illegible]
BIRMINGHAM [illegible]
Tel. [illegible]
Fax [illegible]

2. Human Appeal International
PO Box [illegible]
MANCHESTER M16 [illegible]
Tel. 061 227 [illegible]
Fax 061 [illegible]

Children's Relief Fund,
Markfield Conference Centre,
Ratby Lane, Markfield,
LEICESTER LE67 9RN
Tel. 0530 244145
Fax 0530 244946

APPENDIX VIII

Islamic Bookshops and Resource Centres

1. Islamic Book Centre,
   120 Drummond Street,
   LONDON NW1 2HL
   Tel. 071 388 0710

2. Muslim Information Services,
   233 Seven Sisters Road,
   LONDON N4 2DA
   Tel. 071 272 5170/263 3071

3. Book Service,
   Islamic Cultural Centre,
   146 Park Road,
   LONDON NW8 7RG
   Tel. 071 724 3363/7

4. Ta Ha Publishers,
   1 Wynne Road,
   LONDON SW9 0BD
   Tel. 071 737 7266

5. Al-Huda Bookshop,
   76–78 Charing Cross Road,
   LONDON WC2H 0BB
   Tel. 071 240 8381

6. Al-Nur Bookshop,
   54 Park Road,
   LONDON NW1 4SH
   Tel. 071 723 5414

7. Al-Saqi Bookshop,
   26 Westbourne Grove,
   LONDON W2 5RH
   Tel. 071 229 8543

8. Islamic Foundation,
   Publications Unit,
   Unit 9,
   The Old Dunlop Factory,
   62 Evington Valley Road,
   LEICESTER LE5 5LJ
   Tel. 0533 734860

9. Muslim Booksellers,
   423 Stratford Road,
   BIRMINGHAM B11 4LB
   Tel. 021 773 8301

10. Islamic Book House,
    179 Anderton Road,
    BIRMINGHAM B11 1ND
    Tel. 021 773 8651

11. Rolex Trading,
    6–8 Hall Field Road,
    BRADFORD BD1 3RG
    Tel. 0274 731 908

12. Rolex Trading Co.,
    81–83 Wilmslow Road,
    Rusholme,
    MANCHESTER M14
    Tel. 061 225 4448

13. Book Centre (UK Mission),
    443 Cheetham Hill Road,
    MANCHESTER M8 7PF
    Tel. 061 740 3351

14. Islamic Book Centre,
    19 Carrington Street,
    GLASGOW G4
    Tel. 041 331 119

15. Islamic Book Centre,
    4–8 Forest Street,
    NELSON, Lancashire
    Tel. 0282 694 471

16. Darul Hijrah,
    187 Dickenson Road,
    Longsight,
    MANCHESTER M13 0YW
    Tel. 061 224 0265

Index